HANDLING TOUGH JOB INTERVIEWS

Be prepared, perform well, get the job

**REVISED AND UPDATED
3RD EDITION**

Julie-Ann Amos

howtobooks

Published by How To Books Ltd,
Spring Hill House, Spring Hill Road, Begbroke
Oxford OX5 1RX, United Kingdom.
Tel: (01865) 375794. Fax: (01865) 379162.
info@howtobooks.co.uk
www.howtobooks.co.uk

First edition 2001
Second edition 2004
Reprinted 2005
Third edition 2007

British Library Cataloguing in Publication Data.
A catalogue record for this book is available from
the British Library.

ISBN 978 1 84528 229 5

Produced for How To Books by Deer Park Productions, Tavistock
Typeset by Kestrel Data, Exeter
Cover design by Baseline Arts Ltd, Oxford
Printed and bound by Cromwell Press Ltd, Trowbridge, Wiltshire

NOTE: The material contained in this book is set out in good
faith for general guidance and no liability can be accepted
for loss or expense incurred as a result of relying in particular
circumstances on statements made in the book. Laws and
regulations are complex and liable to change, and readers should
check the current position with the relevant authorities before
making personal arrangements.

HANDLING TOUGH JOB INTERVIEWS

If you want to know how . . .

Be Prepared!
Getting Ready for Job Interviews

Planning a Career Change
Rethink your way to a better working life

High Powered CVs
Powerful application strategies to get you that senior level job

Management Level Psychometric Tests
Everything you need to help you land that senior job

howtobooks

Please send for a free copy of the latest catalogue:
How To Books
Spring Hill House, Spring Hill Road, Begbroke
Oxford OX5 1RX, United Kingdom
info@howtobooks.co.uk
www.howtobooks.co.uk

Contents

Preface

Job interviews can be daunting, because often there is our very livelihood at stake. A little preparation and understanding about how interviews work can help. Even better is understanding the purpose of the different stages of interview in the recruitment process, and where the balance of power in those interviews lies.

This book is not about manipulating interviews, or quick hints to pass difficult ones – although you will receive knowledge that will help you get through the worst of them. It is about understanding why you are there, and what to do when things get difficult. It's about knowing your way through the recruitment process so that each hurdle is cleared to get you the job you want – if it's right for you.

Julie-Ann Amos

1

Introduction

THE JOB INTERVIEW PROCESS

The job interview process can be really confusing. Sometimes, you face a baffling series of interviews with a whole assortment of people, and from the outside it can be very hard to see why people are asking the questions they do.

The huge variety of experiences

There are limitless numbers of interviews and interviewers with which you could be faced. So how can you make it easier on yourself?

First of all, you need to bear in mind that interviewers are only human: there are some very good ones, and quite frankly, some appalling ones! A person may be interviewing you in a certain way purely because they don't know how to interview properly – sometimes it can be as simple as that.

In addition, even given the differences in interviewers' skill and experience, organisations themselves vary in their recruitment processes. Larger organisations tend to have a standard process of interviews before a decision is made. Smaller organisations tend to be more ad hoc – with whoever has most time doing the interviewing, then an interview with the owner or manager.

The structure of this book

The aim of this book is to de-mystify the various interviews and assessments you may be faced with, and to help you get through the process. Because recruitment and interview processes vary so widely, a chapter is devoted to each possible interview or assessment you may face. That way, whatever the process, all you need to ask is:

◆ Who is the person interviewing you?

◆ What is their role?

That will help you to understand the point of that interview, where they are coming from and what they might be looking for. This will help you decide how best to handle it.

Obviously no one can cover every single potential question or give advice on the best response: although many books available do help with this. This book gives general advice and there is a section at the end giving difficult questions with which you may be faced.

A word of warning

Please remember that getting through an interview is only one stage of the recruitment process. And even if you get the job, you then have to work at this organisation for some time. So lying, or trying to appear someone other than yourself, is never a good idea.

Lying or falsifying anything during recruitment is almost always grounds for gross misconduct and possibly dismissal if you are found out – even if you have been working at an organisation for some time. It may get you through the interview. It may get you the job. It may also ultimately lose you the job and blot your employment record, affecting how easy it is to get another.

If you are honest, and are thinking at this point that all this talk of being truthful at interview is unnecessary, that people just don't do this, you might be interested to know that the Chartered Institute of Personnel and Development (CIPD) estimates that one in eight people exaggerate or falsify their qualifications!

Being a different personality for an interview is also never the best plan. Being very quiet and conventional, for example, may make a good impression. But remember, people hire you because they believe you will fit in. Can you keep up your interview act for ever? If you can't, and you eventually revert to being your true self, you will inevitably fall into trouble at work.

YOUR LEGAL RIGHTS

Legally, you do have some rights during the recruitment process. The law protects you from discrimination on the grounds of:

◆ being pregnant

◆ having children

◆ marital status

◆ race or ethnic origin

◆ religion or beliefs

◆ age

◆ sex/gender

◆ sexual orientation

◆ disability.

Let's look at how the law affects you in the recruitment/
interview process.

Criminal records

More than five million people in the UK have convictions
that could have involved imprisonment; one in three men
under the age of 30. If this applies to you, you can regard any
conviction as 'spent' provided that:

◆ it didn't carry a sentence excluded from the Rehabilitation of Offenders Act 1974, such as a custodial sentence
of over 2.5 years, or

◆ no further convictions occurred during the rehabilitation
period as defined in the Act.

Once a conviction is regarded as 'spent' you do not have
to reveal its existence, and can say 'no' if you are asked
whether you have a criminal record. Certain occupations are
exceptions to this, and you would need to check. Helpful
addresses can be found at the back of this book.

Disability

The Disability Discrimination Act 1995 means that if you
have a disability, you have the right not to be discriminated

against because of your disability (as long as the prospective employer has more than 15 employees – smaller companies are exempt).

Race/ethnic origin

Being treated less favourably than others on racial grounds is direct discrimination. There is no justification in law for this, and if a complaint is made, the onus is on the employer to prove this did not occur. Indirect discrimination is more difficult to define, but it exists where a smaller proportion of your sex or race could comply with a requirement of the recruiter, and you are disadvantaged because you can't comply.

Exceptions
There are exceptions, and these are very specific. These exceptions are called GOQs, or Genuine Occupational Qualifications.

Religion or beliefs

Discrimination (direct or indirect) on the grounds of religion or beliefs is unlawful under the Employment Equality (Religion or Belief) Regulations 2003.

Age

Discrimination on age grounds is unlawful under the Employment Equality (Age) Regulations 2006. Employers should be especially careful to avoid implications of age discrimination, such as the use of terms such as 'mature', 'recent graduate', 'young', 'highly experienced', etc.

Sex/gender
Exactly the same applies as for race/ethnic origin above.

Exceptions/GOQs
Examples might include jobs where a particular sex is required for authenticity, eg for an acting role. They also include jobs where a particular sex is required for decency, eg a changing room or toilet attendant.

Pregnancy
A special element of sexual discrimination rights is that European law prohibits discrimination on the grounds of pregnancy.

Marital status
Discrimination on the grounds of marital status is also unlawful.

Sexual orientation
Discrimination on grounds of sexual orientation is unlawful under the Employment Equality (Sexual Orientation) Regulations 2003. Direct or indirect discrimination is covered.

BEST PRACTICE
There are a number of organisations that govern best practice within the UK. The Recruitment and Employment Confederation (REC) has a large number of members – recruitment and employment consultants, agencies and consultancies. Their website, *http://www.rec.uk.com/* gives advice and guidance.

The Chartered Institute of Personnel and Development (CIPD) is the professional organisation for personnel and human resources practitioners. It produces a number of advice notes and publications, and a great deal of information can be found on their website, at *http://www.cipd.co.uk.*

Full details on employment legislation can be found at *http://www.berr.gov.uk/employment/discrimination/index.html.*

HANDLING NERVES

Nervousness and a certain amount of trepidation are natural before an interview. But there are ways you can help yourself, so that you don't let your nerves get in the way of giving a good performance at interview.

Mental solutions

Relax
Telling yourself to relax is easier said than done, but do try. Take deep breaths. Have a relaxing bath or shower before you set off. Stop and have a tea or coffee on the way – whatever works for you (except alcohol!).

Thought patterns
Be aware of thought patterns that may make you even more nervous. Thoughts which induce self-doubt or self-blame, such as these typical examples, never help:

◆ 'Do I look OK in this?'

◆ 'I should have got my hair cut.'

- 'I don't stand a chance.'

- 'What if . . .'

- 'I knew I should have worn . . .'

Once you have set off for the interview it is too late to change things anyway, so just try to let these thoughts go, and think positive.

Think positive

This doesn't mean thinking rosy thoughts, and not bothering to prepare yourself. But do be realistic. If the organisation wasn't interested in you they wouldn't have asked you to an interview, so you must have a reasonable chance. Assume that you will be one of the best people they interview – this will give you confidence.

Physical solutions

Preparation

Get there on time. Allow plenty of time, and then have a coffee, or take a short walk beforehand to calm yourself. There's nothing worse than arriving hot and sticky from a mad rush to get there just in the nick of time. It makes you flustered, and then it can be hard to relax and make a good impression. Give yourself time to make sure you've visited the loo, and checked details like hair, etc.

Reduce distractions

The fewer things you have to worry about, the better. Try to take as little as possible with you, and ask if you can leave what you do take in reception. Often, reception areas in buildings or offices will allow you to leave bags, briefcases and coats with them, if you just ask. That way you can walk into the interview without any distractions, and greet your interviewer(s) without having to juggle hands, take off a coat etc.

Sleep

Get a good night's sleep the night before. You can rarely do your best when you are tired, and if nothing else, it can make you *look* tired, and less alert. You also make more mistakes when you're tired, so do aim to get some quality rest and sleep beforehand.

Alcohol and drugs

A swift drink may calm your nerves, but it can also ruin your chances. Many organisations have a strict no drinking policy during working hours, and even if you have fresh breath they may smell it on your clothes. Similarly, don't be tempted by even a herbal relaxant. Many of them require regular use before the effects build up, so a tablet or two before the interview won't have much effect anyway.

Stopping in a smoky place (whether or not you smoke) can make your hair and clothes smell of cigarette smoke. Non-smoking interviewers may find this unpleasant.

Get support

If you're really nervous, get someone like a friend to go with you and wait outside. They can give you a boost and get your confidence up before you go in. Just having someone to talk to before and afterwards can help put you at ease.

Practice

Rehearse your technique. Get someone to ask you interview questions from your CV or application form, and practise giving answers until you are happy with them. Obviously, the more experienced someone is in your line of work, the better they will be able to advise you.

DECIDING WHAT TO WEAR

Many people have trouble deciding what to wear. Regardless of whether or not the company has a relaxed dress policy, looking smart is rarely out of place. Your clothes are a way of communicating with the interviewer just as much as what you tell him or her in words.

Generally speaking, business dress for men is becoming more colourful and less traditional. For women, it is becoming less tailored and traditional. But taking a gamble by wearing something unusual may not pay off. You need to create a balance between what you prefer to wear, and what the interviewer is likely to expect.

For the best chance of success, play it safe: nothing too formal, or too casual. The golden rules are that dress should be:

◆ appropriate for the job or organisation

◆ flattering

◆ clean and tidy

◆ comfortable

◆ a reflection of your personality

◆ clothing that gives you confidence.

Detail *is* important – for example, scuffed shoes, untidy hair, dirty fingernails etc are all standard black marks with interviewers! Use common sense, get a second opinion if necessary, and don't worry about it too much.

Always check things like buttons, zips etc at the last minute – there's nothing worse than finding they don't work just before walking into the building!

Make sure clothes are comfortable. You may not be aware of it, but your whole body language and facial expressions can change if you're uncomfortable. Tight shoes, waistbands too tight, straps that rub – all these things can make you look strained and ill at ease, which can give a negative impression.

THE START OF THE INTERVIEW

People say that the first 30 seconds are when the decision is made. Although this isn't quite true, this is usually the time when the interviewer makes up his or her mind about you in many ways. Think about what actually happens in the first 30 seconds of an interview. In this short period of time you are likely to be:

◆ knocking on a door

◆ seeing the interviewer(s) for the first time

- walking in

- saying hello

- shaking hands

- taking off a coat

- sitting down

- accepting or declining water, tea or coffee.

Wow! A lot goes on, doesn't it? And in this short space of time people make decisions about what they think of you. So each of these things is important.

Making the entrance

Don't be too timid. A shaky tap on a door sometimes gets ignored, as people aren't sure if someone was there or not. Be sensible, and give a businesslike knock. Don't wait by the door, hovering uncertainly! Walk in, and go towards the interviewer to shake hands and say hello. This shows confidence in yourself, and helps if the interviewer is nervous as well. If you are asked to wait in the room for the interviewer, you will be there already when they come in. Simply stand up, and move towards them to shake hands. Whatever you do, don't hover, standing up until they arrive – this will only make you look nervous and it could be a long wait.

Seeing the interviewer(s) for the first time

So now you can see the monster about whom you've been nervous! Look them in the eye and smile. If they look away from you, keep looking at them – and keep smiling. Say hello, and offer your hand to shake – don't wait for them to shake hands. Do make sure you shake hands sensibly. No one wants their knuckles cracked, but neither does a limp soggy handshake do anything for your image. You actually need to take hold of the person's hand and shake it – once. At the same time, introduce yourself if this hasn't already happened. Say something simple like: 'Julie-Ann Amos, nice to meet you', with a smile. To do all this you need to be ready, and have put bags, briefcases etc down or have them in your left hand to leave your right hand free. Or ideally, leave them outside with reception, as we said earlier.

Getting settled

There now follows something that should be very simple, but can in reality be very awkward: sitting down and taking off a coat if you are wearing one. Sit down when you're invited to – it's sometimes seen as bad-mannered if you just sit down without waiting to be asked. When the interviewer says 'take a seat', remember to say thank you. It's not just polite, it fills the silence and dialogue helps to break the ice.

Get relaxed and comfortable. Fidgeting during the interview almost always creates a bad impression, so get yourself settled now.

Refreshments

People get very nervous about having tea, coffee or water during the interview. Basically, there's nothing much to worry about. If there's nothing visible and you're asked, the best option is probably to say, 'if you're having something I'll join you, but otherwise I'm fine, thank you.' This means there's no need for the interviewer to order something specially, which can take time and make the atmosphere strained. If drinks are there in the room, it is perfectly safe to say, 'yes please' and have one. The only thing you should avoid at all costs is biscuits – it's very hard to answer questions with your mouth full!

Breaking the ice

Most interviewers have a few questions ready at the beginning, to break the ice and put you at your ease. Be careful how you answer them. Often people ask questions such as, 'so did you find us OK' or 'how was the journey?'. *Never* tell them you had any problem getting there – if you get the job you'll have to do that journey every day, remember! So make sure they don't have any reason to think it would be difficult for you.

Another favourite warm-up question is to ask whether you're okay for time. This is asking whether or not you have to leave by a certain time, for example to get back to work. Be careful not to say that you've gone sick for the day, or are in any other way deceiving your current employer. It looks dishonest, and interviewers may assume that you would do this to them if you got the job – it can put some interviewers off. Just beware of giving anything other than a good impression.

BODY LANGUAGE

In many ways, the subject of body language is enough to fill a book in itself – and it has, many times! But before you rush out and buy one, remember that there is so much information and advice on body language available that it can be very bewildering. Here are some solid hints, listed from your head downwards, that will make sure you don't go far wrong.

Head

Smile, and don't look too serious and nervous. Even a nervous smile is better than gritted teeth! Look at the interviewer – eye contact is one of the most important things people notice. Nod when you agree with them. Try to keep an interested expression when they are talking.

Upper body

Don't lean too far back, or slouch – it looks over-casual. Don't lean forward too much either. It can look good to lean forward when making a point, but beware of appearing too forceful or eager.

Hands

It's better not to fold your arms – it signals to the vast majority of people that you are unapproachable and uncomfortable. After all, your arms make a physical barrier between you and the interviewer. Find a relaxed position for your hands – resting casually in your lap, or one hand in the other – whatever you feel comfortable with. Don't be afraid to use your hands when making a point, but beware of waving them about too much, as it can be distracting.

Lower body

Just do what feels comfortable with your legs. Cross them or not, but don't stick them out in front of you. If you do cross your legs, beware of crossing them and uncrossing them several times. This only makes you look nervous, uncomfortable and fidgety. Try to avoid sitting with your legs wide apart! This applies to men and women alike.

Mirroring

Mirroring is a simple technique where one person mimics or mirrors another's body language. It usually helps two people to feel comfortable with each other. Doing this subtly and slowly with an interviewer can establish a good relationship. But you must beware of being obvious – if they lean back and cross their legs, wait a short while then do this yourself, as if it just happened naturally. The whole idea is to not be noticed, but to put the other person at ease, so they feel you are someone they can really get to know and like.

ASKING QUESTIONS

At the end of the interview, the interviewers usually ask whether you have any questions. This is a somewhat sticky area for many interviewees, as they aren't sure what to say.

Prepare

If possible, prepare in advance. Have one or two questions ready, so that when you are asked if you have any, you can appear both intelligent and interested by asking something. You don't have to use the ones you've prepared – if something better occurs to you during the interview, ask that instead. But if you're short of ideas, showing an interest in the organisation and its plans for the future is a great idea.

Questions to avoid

Avoid questions that make it appear you are concerned about joining them. So don't ask about:

◆ possible takeovers

◆ the risk of redundancy

◆ potential closure.

Try also to avoid questions that make it appear as if you have reservations – so do not ask questions such as:

◆ Would I have to be involved in . . .

◆ Is it a problem if . . .

◆ How important is it that I . . .

Finally, avoid specific questions about terms and conditions and salary until the appropriate stage – which is usually not the first interview. Many interviewers want to make their mind up first, and then worry about the potential deal later. Asking about money at too early a stage makes you seem money-oriented, which a lot of people dislike.

Safe questions

◆ The organisation's recent news, if there has been any.

◆ Plans for expansion.

◆ What is the recruitment process following this interview – what would be the next stage?

◆ Is this a new role or was there a previous person doing it?

◆ Where is the previous post-holder now? (It can be useful knowing whether the previous person was promoted, transferred, or left.)

Never

◆ Say you have no questions if you can possibly avoid it.

◆ Ask whether you have got the job.

◆ Ask how the interviewer feels about the interview or your application.

THE END OF THE INTERVIEW

Once the interview is over you have to get out gracefully. The process of getting up, gathering your possessions, shaking hands, opening the door and getting away can be a very jumbled and clumsy period. It can even be easy to undo a good interview by saying something through nerves and relief. Candidates have been known to say 'well, I'm glad that's over,' or 'I can relax now,' even 'I hope you find the right person for the job!' It's surprising how some people react!

Getting out is just as important as making your entrance. Stand up, gather your things, smile, lean over or walk over and shake hands, and head for the door. When you shake hands it's good to simply say 'it was nice meeting you'. Avoid 'thank you for your time,' or 'I hope to see you again' – keep it simple, to leave a good last impression. Don't apologise on the way out – remember that the last thing you say makes an impression, so don't leave the interviewer with the impression that you feel guilty for wasting their time!

CHECKLIST

◆ Never falsify information or lie to an interviewer.

◆ Take steps to control your nerves as much as possible.

◆ Dress sensibly and comfortably.

◆ Make a professional entrance and exit.

◆ Don't carry baggage or clothing if possible – keep clutter at home.

◆ Practise a decent handshake.

◆ Smile, and keep eye contact.

◆ Be aware of your body language.

◆ Prepare questions to ask, and always ask something.

◆ Give at least as much thought to leaving the room as you do to entering it.

2

Interviews with Recruitment Agencies

THE PURPOSE OF THE INTERVIEW

When dealing with a recruitment agency, you have to be aware of *why* they are interviewing you. There are several possible scenarios:

◆ You may have approached them, looking for a job.

◆ You may have answered an advertisement and they are handling the job.

◆ You may have applied to a particular company, and the agency handles the company's recruitment.

◆ You may have left your details on an Internet site and they are contacting you.

◆ They may have contacted you out of the blue. This is commonly referred to as head-hunting, and will be dealt with in the next chapter.

Basically, we can split these into two main reasons:

1 They are interviewing you generally, as part of their process of registering you onto their database of candidates.

2 They are interviewing you in connection with either

◆ a specific position or

◆ a specific company which has a vacancy.

General interviews

Surprisingly, not all recruitment agencies interview you before accepting you onto their pool of candidates, and this is something you should give some thought to. If you were a company looking for a member of staff, would you be happy for an agency to send candidates to you for interview, if you knew the agency had never seen them? How could that agency possibly know whether you are presentable, can communicate with others, can fulfil the requirements of the job etc, without meeting you?

Most companies either make it a requirement that candidates from agencies have been seen by the agency, or they assume that this has been done. An agency that just accepts your CV and then starts trying to match you with companies cannot ever be as professional as one that gets to know you, and sees what sort of person you are, so that they can assess where you would enjoy working.

Establishing a relationship
To get the best service as a candidate you need to establish a relationship with your agency, so that you can be confident they will be able to find you suitable employment openings. If they just send you for an interview with a company or client without having seen you, you have to ask yourself whether they themselves have done something similar with the job on offer – have they really a good understanding of

what that job entails? How well do they know you? How well do they know the job? Can you be sure that they are matching you with a job you will want to do and enjoy doing? It's not very likely.

This general interview *should* be an opportunity for the agency (or at least, your consultant at the agency) to assess you and your personality. They should get a feel for the type of work you like and can do, and the type of organisation where you would fit in and be successful.

Specific interviews

If a recruitment agency asks to see you about a particular job or a specific company, however, then this is really the first hurdle in the recruitment process. You should think of this as the first interview for this job.

THE BALANCE OF POWER

You might think that when you go for *any* interview, the balance of power lies with the interviewer. Not so. When interviewing at a recruitment agency, a lot of power actually rests with you. Recruitment agencies derive their income and profit from placing candidates with employers. Basically, you represent a fee to the agency, and therefore it is to some extent in their own interests to find you a job.

How do they earn their rewards?

There is, however, another consideration. Although if they find you a job the *agency* will earn a fee, the person who interviews you is a consultant, working for the agency. Depending on the agency concerned and the way it pays its staff, consultants can be rewarded in two ways. Most agencies pay a basic salary plus commission or bonus. The relative proportions of commission or bonus in a consultant's pay packet can either be dependent on the number of placements a consultant makes, or on the number of people signed onto the agency's database (or both in some instances).

Consultants paid more for making placements will obviously try hard to find you a job, as you represent income to them personally, as well as the agency. However, agencies that reward consultants mainly for signing up new candidates may have a large database which in no way guarantees you much help in finding a job. In fact, they may make little or no effort to do so, as the consultant is busy making more money by signing up other people, and not finding *you* work.

In any event, an interview with a recruitment agency will usually mean that they are keen to get you onto their database. The interview may not be easy, but it shouldn't be too difficult, and you could get some useful advice for future interviews if you remember to ask for feedback on your performance afterwards.

Who pays the bill?

Always remember, the agency is working for the employer. They may offer you career advice, and some agencies are fantastic at helping you towards finding a really good job. But just be aware that any careers advice an agency gives you may be more in line with their commercial intentions as to what they want you to do, rather than what is actually best for you right now. Always remember that the employer pays their fee, not you.

MAKING THE RIGHT IMPRESSION

So how can you make the best impression at an interview with a recruitment agency? Remember, the agency is looking at you as a potential fee. The more jobs they can match your skills and experience with, the more likely they are to get you a job, and gain their fee.

Making the best impression with an agency, therefore, may mean being flexible. The more roles you are happy to consider, and the more companies, the better. Candidates who only want to work in banking, or who only want to do administration but don't want a job involving filing, are limiting their options.

As well as being flexible, be interested and proactive. Impress on the agency that you are keen to work and to progress your career, and they will see you as motivated and therefore easier to place.

Dress well, so the agency knows that they can send you to any of their clients with confidence. It can be tempting to think it's 'only an agency', especially if you have already done the rounds of several agency interviews. But dressing inappropriately may well put them off sending you to important clients for an interview, in case you let them down.

ESSENTIALS TO GET ACROSS

You are worth their effort

The essential fact to get across to a recruitment agency is that you will represent a good investment for them; that any time spent in marketing you to their clients will be likely to result in you performing well at interview and earning them a fee.

Financial requirements

You also want them to be very sure of your financial requirements. When clients come to them with a job they will be briefed as to the likely salary – whether or not they tell *you* what that is! So you want to be sure that you are only sent to interviews for jobs that will meet your financial needs. It's a waste of time going to interviews for jobs that pay less than you need. When going via an agency you aren't in control of the recruitment process, and you often don't know the salary for the job, unlike when you respond to an advert.

Flexibility

Make sure the agency knows what you might consider, as well as your ideal move. We all have ideal jobs, but we usually also have other things that we would consider, so bring them into the equation. This means that you will possibly be matched with a wider number of vacancies, and more likely to get a job. If you are *not* willing to take a particular type of job, be open about it, or you may waste a great deal of time later being sent to interviews for jobs that are of no interest to you.

Limiting factors

Of course if you do have limiting factors, such as being unable to work late, or that you can't work weekends, let them know. It looks bad for both you and the agency if it comes to light at interview with an employer that you cannot fulfil an essential part of the job. It's demoralising for you, and the agency may suffer loss of reputation with that client.

Your own requirements

Be firm about what you are looking for – what you do and don't want. Ask the agency to check all jobs with you first *before* submitting your CV. This ensures, of course, that you only get put forward for jobs that you have agreed are of interest to you. This should prevent your time being wasted. According to REC, the Recruitment Employment Confederation (the industry body for recruitment consultants and employment agencies), standard practice for all its members is to ensure that candidates agree to each application for a role that the agency or consultant makes on your behalf. Recruitment consultants may get you the job you want. They may also try to get you to take the job they are trying to fill. Just be wary and hopefully you will be dealing with reputable agencies, so you will have nothing to be concerned about.

QUESTIONS TO ASK

How many vacancies do you have at present?

It is useful to assess how many vacancies they have. This gives you an idea of how quickly they may be able to get you an interview with one of their clients. You could also ask how many of them you might be right for, to check how well they can help you with your search for a job.

Do you have vacancies at the moment that I might be right for?

It's also useful to know if there is anything *at the moment* which you might be suitable for: if so, you need to be ready for an interview quite quickly. It also helps to know if there's nothing at present, so you aren't waiting for the phone to ring and getting discouraged when it doesn't. If there will be a delay it's better to be aware of it.

How soon will it be before I'm likely to hear from you?

This gives you an idea of when you may be contacted. But it also serves another purpose: you have to remember that, at some agencies, you are one of literally thousands of people on their database. It's easy to be overlooked or forgotten. So get an idea of when they might get back to you, and if they don't, call them for an update. Keeping your name in the consultant's mind is important when you are up against a large database of people competing for a job opportunity when one comes up.

Who is my point of contact?

This is *essential* – some agencies have consultants employed specifically to interview new candidates, but these people aren't the ones who will be dealing with them if and when vacancies arise. So make sure you leave the agency with a point of contact that you can call when you want to know what's going on.

Is there anything else I need to do to maximise my chances of getting a job?

It's very useful to seek advice. If your image needs a bit of a boost, you talk too fast, or if finishing a qualification would greatly increase your chances, you want to know about it *now*. It's too late in six month's time, when they have been unable to find you work and *finally* tell you why. Get advice now and act on it – these people are professionals in placing candidates with employers. Use them and the experience they have in finding people jobs.

What happens now?

Find out what the process is. If it takes a week for them to rewrite your CV and enter it into their system, it's pointless you waiting for a phone call in four days' time. Find out what happens next, and by when.

Can you give me some feedback?

After the interview, if there is time, ask for feedback on your interview performance. If the consultant has another appointment, phone them back the next day and ask. This is all good information about how you perform in an interview, and you can learn from it. These people see hundreds of candidates, after all – this is a golden opportunity to get some useful feedback.

WHAT HAPPENS NOW?

There are a number of possibilities. Basically, the aim of using an agency is for them to get you a job with one of their clients. So the next step would usually be that the agency arranges an interview for you when they have a suitable vacancy with a client.

Sometimes, they might ask you to come back in for a briefing first. It's not unusual for you to go to the agency for a quick briefing and then on to an interview. If not, you may get a phone call to brief you. Getting a briefing is a very good thing – the more information you have about the job, the better your chances of giving a good interview when you get there.

CHECKLIST

◆ Dress to impress.

◆ Don't be nervous – this isn't usually a job interview, and you can relax and use it as a very useful learning experience.

◆ Be confident – reassure the agency that you will be a good candidate.

◆ Be flexible, to maximise your chances of finding work.

◆ Don't overlook limitations or they will send you to inappropriate interviews.

◆ Ask questions.

◆ Make sure you leave with a point of contact.

◆ Ensure they know your salary limitations.

◆ Get feedback.

3

Interviews with Head-Hunters

THE DIFFERENCE BETWEEN HEAD-HUNTERS AND RECRUITMENT AGENCIES

A true head-hunter is a consultant who approaches you (usually by telephone) and asks you to speak with them about a potential job for which you haven't applied. *They* come to *you*. This is the only type of recruitment situation where you aren't the one in the driving seat – you can't apply to a head-hunter (although you might eventually end up on their database for future openings they handle, if they like you but you don't get the particular job they approached you about).

Head-hunters usually only deal with senior positions – those paying large salaries. But if a particular skill set or combination of skills and/or experience/qualifications is in short supply, they may be used to find just the right person for a job with very specific or unusual requirements.

They are paid by a company to look for the right person for them. They're usually paid a retainer – so they get paid a certain percentage of their fee before they have even started the work! The usual operating process in the UK is that they are paid one-third of the total fee to start work, one-third of the fee when they present a shortlist of candidates to the employer, and one-third when the job is filled.

Head-hunters can be slightly peculiar to work with, in that they can be very secretive. This can be for a number of reasons. They may not be able to tell you who the job is for – which company they are recruiting for. They may have been asked not to by their client. But they also have to exercise some caution, as you represent a potential fee to them. If they tell you which company is looking for your exact skills and experience, you might just contact the company direct, and they'd lose their fee!

One thing to bear in mind is that they are usually looking for something *very specific* for an employer. This means that:

(a) There's no need to feel slighted if you don't get the job – the requirements are usually very precise and hard to find, which is why head-hunters are being used in the first place.

(b) Your chances of getting the job are actually quite low – head-hunters research a large number of people, and only present a few to their client. Just being contacted and interviewed doesn't mean that you are in with a good chance, it means they are trying to find out whether you fit the bill or not. Your chances of success may be a lot less than when being interviewed by a recruitment agency, for example.

(c) On the other hand, you are likely to have a very high chance of getting the job if you progress as far as being interviewed by the company looking for someone. This is because if you get to that stage, it means you are potentially a perfect match with their requirements – you know you are on a very small shortlist.

THE BALANCE OF POWER

In a nutshell, this is one interview where the balance of power rests firmly with the head-hunter on the face of things. They have all the information, whereas you have only as much as they give you, and that's very often none!

Disadvantages

◆ You have no information unless they choose to give it to you.

◆ You can't judge how to present yourself in the best light unless you know what they're looking for.

◆ Even answering very simple questions can eliminate you from the running, if the answer isn't what they are looking for – and you don't know what that is!

Advantages

There are some advantages, though.

◆ You've been head-hunted. Congratulations! You must have something that people want.

◆ If you *are* right for the job, they will be very keen to persuade you to look at it and meet with the employer. So if you do get through the initial interview and progress to meeting the employer, your chances are very good.

THE PURPOSE OF THE INTERVIEW

Skill and expertise

The purpose of an interview with a head-hunter is for them to initially interview you and see whether you are indeed a match for the role they are seeking to fill. They will probably be asking the majority of their questions about the level of skill and experience you have in various areas. Examples might include:

◆ How much experience do you have in cashflow analysis?

◆ In your current role, what percentage of your time is spent in customer contact?

◆ Have you ever done sales presentations?

Ideologically/personality fit

You can also expect to be assessed as to how good a 'fit' you might be with the organisation. Cultural issues, personality and approach may be something they have been asked to look at, to ensure they don't offer a candidate with a very relaxed working style, for example, to a very formal company. Examples of these questions might include:

◆ Would you say that your current employer is a good place to work?

◆ Have you ever worked in a non-profit organisation?

◆ Do you prefer to work in a formal hierarchy or a relaxed organisational structure?

◆ My client is a Japanese company – do you know much about their working style and culture?

Willingness to move jobs right now

The final area which a head-hunter may want to explore is how likely you are to progress things if they think you would be suitable for the job on offer. Bearing in mind the fact that *they* asked *you* to interview, and you didn't apply for the job, there is a chance that you're actually fairly happy where you are currently working and don't want to move.

They do know that you are at least willing to attend an interview, but how serious are you about taking a new job if offered one? It's pointless them presenting you to their client, you interviewing and even being offered the job, if you weren't seriously willing to accept it if offered. They need to assess how you feel about the type of work the job involves, the type of company etc, and be absolutely sure they aren't wasting their client's time.

MAKING THE RIGHT IMPRESSION

When meeting with a head-hunter, you usually want to be carried forward to the next stage of the process. It never pays to be too suspicious. Just try to relax; if they don't give you much information, just let it go and don't be wary or come across as though you might not be very interested. Playing hard to get at this stage is not really a good idea. They won't put forward a candidate they think will be difficult when interviewing with their client, after all.

You need to convey the impression that you're open to the right offer if anything suitable comes up; and that you're happy where you're working at present if anything doesn't. Don't appear desperate to move, because if you're unhappy where you are, why aren't you already looking for yourself?

As you can't tell exactly what skills and/or experience they are looking for (unless they choose to tell you), there's no point trying to bluff about how experienced you arc. You could be telling them you're experienced at something which you really enjoy, but that is something that they *aren't* looking for! Just be honest. If you're asked in detail about experience you don't have much of, say so now.

Being honest

Give an accurate account of your abilities and the experience you have. Be honest about any gaps you have – if you have no experience in a particular area, say so when asked. Far better to eliminate yourself from their search at this stage than progress things further and ending up embarrassing them – they won't represent you again if you do that. You may not be put forward for this job, but at least the head-hunter knows he or she can trust you, and they may find you suitable for something else at a later date.

QUESTIONS TO ASK

Can you give me any more information?

The most obvious question to ask is what the job is and who the employer is. The head-hunter may not tell you, but at least you should ask. If nothing else, you should try to establish whether the job is a promotion from the role you currently do, and what type of business the employer is in.

Have I been successful?

Obviously you wouldn't put it like that, but basically when you leave, it's useful to know whether the head-hunter thinks you might be a suitable match or not. Ask directly, 'do you mind if I ask whether or not you think I am a good fit with what you're looking for?' Usually they will say if you are, and if not, head-hunters tend to say something like, 'possibly, but I need to have a think about it and see one or two other people. I'll get back to you.' It saves you becoming excited about what was, after all, an unexpected opportunity if you aren't right for the job.

What sort of salary/package is on offer?

You might think that no head-hunter or recruitment agency would put you forward for a job paying the same or even less than you earn now, wouldn't you? All I can say is that stranger things have happened! Best to ask the question now.

What skills/competencies are you looking for?

If you could ask this at the beginning, you'd get a real feel for what they are looking for! In any event, it gives you a little more idea of whether or not you'd be interested.

WHAT HAPPENS NOW?

The process after an interview with a head-hunter may well be slightly longer than you are used to. Remember, this first interview is merely designed to see whether or not you should go on a shortlist to the client. The typical head-hunter is different from a recruitment agency, in that unlike the agency the head-hunter has to interview every single candidate before deciding whether or not to place them on the shortlist. This can take time, especially if you are one of the first to be interviewed, before you hear anything else. An agency, on the other hand, may have interviewed you once, and can then put you forward for jobs without interviewing you again. So things have a tendency to move much more quickly.

Then once the shortlist goes from the head-hunter to the client there may be a further delay whilst the employer decides who to interview. So don't worry if things seem a little slow.

After that the process is that the employer may decide:

◆ You aren't right for them – in which case the head-hunter will let you know.

◆ They'd like to see you – in which case the head-hunter should arrange an interview.

Remember, the interview with the employer means that you are in with a very good chance, as you have been very thoroughly screened against their precise requirements. There may be further, subsequent interviews at the company, but processes vary.

CHECKLIST

◆ Remember how head-hunters work.

◆ Relax and enjoy yourself. You've been head-hunted, and that means you have skills and experience that someone wants!

◆ Be honest – you can't fake this interview and trot out the desired answer to a question – you don't usually know what they're looking for!

◆ Don't relax too much – playing hard to get may make a head-hunter nervous of putting you in front of a client.

◆ Do check the salary on offer. Unless this is discussed you may end up being put forward for a role which pays little or nothing more than you currently earn – or even less! The secrecy surrounding head-hunting can mean that salary mismatches occur.

4

Employer Interviews

THE PURPOSE OF THE INTERVIEW

Agency versus direct application

This chapter will cover interviews with a prospective employer. By this we are referring to interviews with the actual organisation or company, not with an agency or head-hunter. This may of course be the first interview for you, if you have applied to the company direct and not gone through a recruitment agency or head-hunter.

You may have applied to the company for the job in response to hearing about it from an external source – i.e. an advertisement in the newspaper, a magazine, or even online. Alternatively you may have applied direct to the company asking whether they had any potentially suitable vacancies (applying 'on-spec').

The only real difference in meeting an employer at interview is in how much information you will have. Usually, if you have applied via an agency or head-hunter, they will have briefed you to some extent (and often very comprehensively) about their client, the company, the job itself and any relevant personalities. If you have applied direct you may well not have any of this information, but try not to worry, and certainly don't let that put you off – remember, the information given to you by any agency is only second-, or even third-hand. It isn't always accurate, and the employer should understand that you may have limited information.

Making a decision

Regardless of how you arrived here, this is your first interview with the employer themselves – the first time you will be meeting someone from the company concerned. The purpose of this interview for both parties will always be to decide whether or not to progress your application any further. That means both of you! The employer is trying to decide whether to progress your application, and you should also be assessing whether or not you would really want to work there.

Let's face it, work is somewhere you spend a large percentage of your waking time, so don't waste time pursuing jobs that you wouldn't want to do anyway. Job-hunting is a time-consuming process. You only have so much time you can allow for interviews, especially if you are currently working and have to take time off for interviews without your current employer knowing. You certainly don't want to waste precious time interviewing for jobs you don't want – although a little practice if you haven't been interviewed for a while might be a good thing!

Assessing the 'fit'
So this first interview is really a little bit like a blind date – assessing whether there is a potential 'fit' between the two parties. It may be that the employer really liked your

application or CV and thinks you may be right for their role. It may also be that they aren't sure about your suitability at all, but they wanted to meet you in person to evaluate your application and expand on the experience in your CV. If you return for subsequent interviews, this would indicate that they are interested in you, and are trying to decide whether or not they should hire you.

Personnel or human resources (HR)

In some companies, personnel or human resources (HR) interview first. In others, they interview as one of the last steps in the recruitment process. In some companies they don't interview at all. Just be aware of this – the next chapter deals with personnel or HR interviews.

THE BALANCE OF POWER

In this situation, the balance of power is actually about equal – *it just doesn't feel like it*! Given that you and the employer are both assessing each other to some extent, the balance of power is actually fairly evenly distributed. What changes the balance of power is how badly you want/need the job – how badly you want to progress to the next stage. The more you want or need the job, the more the balance of power shifts to the employer.

Sometimes, we get into an interview and feel very under-confident – perhaps the interviewer is giving you signs that they feel you aren't right for the job, or perhaps you just feel very nervous. In an interview where you feel under-confident, it can often be useful to remember that *you* are checking *them* out as well. This can make you feel a lot better and more confident. You do have some power – after all, they need someone, and you are both available and interested – and also perhaps ideal for the job!

MAKING THE RIGHT IMPRESSION

Positive impressions

Physical impressions
Dress smartly as always. All the advice from Chapter 1 on the usual things, such as arriving on time etc apply here.

Interest and enthusiasm
Be clearly interested in the company. This is where you will be working if you get the job, so appear interested and enthusiastic about it. Even if it isn't the most exciting job in the world, the employer wants to know you aren't wasting their time, so be positive.

Subtle factors
Be nice to everybody! It is so easy to be focused on the interview that you forget to be pleasant to the receptionist or security guard; or you barge into a lift full of people, in a hurry to get to the reception area or interview on time. You never know who people are, or who can see and hear you. From the moment you enter the building you may be under scrutiny, so think what feedback might result. Treat everyone with the respect you give to your interviewer, wherever in the company you encounter them.

Keep a positive attitude

Don't be yourself – be yourself giving your very best performance on a good day! This doesn't mean being totally positive, but don't dwell on failures and negative experiences, even if asked. Focus on positive elements of your personality, CV and experience, and if you are asked to give a negative answer, such as to give an example of a decision you made and later regretted, or a weak point, make these work for you too.

Answering negative questions

Sometimes interviewers ask you to describe a failure, your greatest weakness, or a negative experience in some way. Always do this when asked, and don't say 'I can't think of one' as this only sounds glib and evasive. Let's face it, everyone makes mistakes, so it sounds suspicious if you suddenly can't remember any of yours! Give the appropriate answer or example, but end on a positive note. You can always end on a positive by mentioning what you learned from it, how you improved/changed because of it, or even what you now know you need to do differently next time. It's good to think of a few things beforehand that you can discuss, such as weaknesses and failures in the past that are now resolved. That way, you always have a ready answer.

Preparation

For most employers, how much you have prepared for an interview is a guideline that shows how keen you are about the job. Preparation also increases your confidence – it makes it easier for you to *feel* ready for whatever questions they ask. *Never* go into an interview 'cold' – i.e. unprepared.

If nothing else, taking some company information with you shows that you have taken the interview seriously.

So how much preparation should you do? Basically, imagine that every employer you meet will ask you, 'So what do you know about the company?' and prepare accordingly – you won't go far wrong.

Research

There are a number of sources of information on the company:

◆ Recruitment agencies may be able to brief you.

◆ Careers services.

◆ Local libraries.

◆ The company personnel department – phone and ask them if they have any company literature, as you are coming for an interview.

◆ The Internet. Try *search engines*, which enable you to search for up-to-date news on companies by name.

ESSENTIALS TO GET ACROSS

Let's think this through. If an employer found you were missing skills or experience he or she needed, you wouldn't get the job. That would not be your fault, it's just that you aren't a good fit for that particular job's requirements. But excluding not having the skills/experience necessary, the main reasons for employers not offering candidates the job can be a little surprising.

The interviewer's three main concerns

Reasons for not hiring a person can more often than not be based around what we could call the interviewer's 'three main concerns'. They may not even be aware that they are concerned about these things – they may be totally unconscious worries. These are:

1. Do you really want the job?
Because if not, they are wasting their time and possibly losing other candidates by pursuing you.

2. Would you fit in?
Because if not, things might go wrong and cause more problems.

3. Would you stay?
Because if not, they will have to go through this recruitment all over again in a few years or even months.

So assuming that you *do* have the skills for the job, you need to convince the interviewer that you want it, you would fit in well and you'd stay a reasonable length of time before looking for pastures new.

Do you see how you can maximise your chances of doing well by making sure you address these three concerns?

Addressing the three main concerns

Basically, employers are reassured by candidates who exhibit these three things. Many interview questions reflect these three areas of concern, although the reason they are asked may be entirely different. Yet the answers you choose to give may give the interviewer a picture of someone who doesn't want the job very much, who might not fit in, or who wouldn't stay. This can lose you the job.

For example, a fairly common question is; 'where do you see yourself in five years' time?' Interviewers seem to ask this to see whether you are ambitious or not. Many candidates, not wishing to appear unambitious, say, 'in a much more senior role.' Now there's nothing wrong with this answer, but it all adds to the impression the interviewer may be picking up about concern three – whether you would stay.

Another example would be if you are asked 'why are you looking for a new role at this particular time?' This is probably asked because they are trying to see whether you have any negative reasons for moving – i.e. you've had a bad appraisal, or you're worried about your company declining. By responding with something like, 'I'm in no rush really, I'm happy where I am, but would like more of a challenge so I thought I'd test the market' you are raising concern one – do you really want the job?

At one time, a common interview question used to be 'so if we offered you the job, would you take it?' That's very much testing concern one, isn't it? The only correct answer is 'yes; from what I've heard so far I'm very interested' or words to that effect. 'I'd have to think it through' on the other hand, although a perfectly valid answer, may well blow your chances of being offered the job or taken through to the next stage of the recruitment process.

Now that this question isn't used as often by interviewers, don't think that the concern isn't there. Try to impress upon the interviewer that you would accept the job if offered it. It certainly can't do you any harm to give this impression

QUESTIONS TO ASK

Can you tell me what skills or competencies are the most important to be successful in this job?

This may seem like a strange question. After all, the employer must think you have the necessary skills/ experience, in order for them to have decided to interview you. You may even find that the interviewer has given you a run-down on the job as part of the interview. That's okay, you are asking what the *most important* parts of their requirements are. Why?

Well, if they tell you what is most important to them, it gives you an opportunity to highlight your expertise in this area. You should ask the question because it enables you to focus their attention on your suitability. When they tell you, you can say something like 'that's interesting. I don't think my CV shows just how much of my time at JB Jones was spent on that type of work. I've always found it fascinating.'

What would be the best and worst points of this position?

This is a good question from two points of view. First, it's good to ask if you have any doubts whatsoever over whether or not you are interested. It's also another opportunity to shine. If they tell you the worst points of the job, and you can say 'Is that all? I find I actually *like* that kind of task', it tells them that you'd be a good fit with the job, and that you would probably stay – going back to the three fundamental concerns of interviewers.

Would you be the person I report to? If not, will I be able to meet him or her?

This question first tells you if this would be your new boss, so that you can judge whether or not you'd like working for them. But secondly, and more importantly, it forces the interviewer to picture you as an employee – they have to either imagine themselves as your boss, or imagine someone else at the company as your boss. Seeing you in the job is a powerful psychological shift, and usually can only be beneficial.

Assuming I took the job, how big a team would I be working with?

Again, the interviewer starts to imagine you in their team. This is a very good move on your part, as imagining important events is something we do all the time. What person starting a new job doesn't imagine their first day, for example? What bride doesn't imagine herself walking down the aisle? It's human nature. Make yourself part of their imagined picture, and they are more likely to feel you are the right person for the job.

What would you say should be my number one priority if I took this job?

This question also forces the interviewer to picture you actually doing the job.

What happens next?

It helps to know how long you are likely to wait before hearing anything. Be warned, however, a lot of interviewers get quite detailed when asked this question, and talk about timescales and deadlines. This can falsely raise your hopes, to be told about future interviews if you aren't invited back, for example. It can also make the interviewer stop thinking about you, and start thinking about the arduous task of recruiting. You become part of a problem, not a possible solution. It's best to leave this question to the very end, and be very casual about it. If the interviewer starts going into the process in detail, just say 'that's fine, I just wanted some idea as to roughly when I can expect to hear from you.'

One last question

Before you say you've no more questions, just think for a moment. This is your one opportunity before the interview ends to 'squeeze in' any information you've not had a chance to offer until now. You can sell yourself just one more time! This is easy to do by a question such as, 'I've had a lot of experience with handling . . . How do you handle those transactions here?' This tells them you've had a lot of experience at it, and draws attention to the thought you've put into the task.

WHAT TO DO WITH HOSTILE INTERVIEWERS

Hostile interviewers – a personal example

Do hostile interviews still happen? Unfortunately, yes. There are still plenty of tales of candidates being harangued by hostile interviewers. To give an example, I have personally been asked as the first question in a job interview, 'I don't know why they want me to see you, I don't need an HR manager, your CV's totally irrelevant to the job – what on earth have you got that I'd be interested in?' Great! It really made me feel like working for that person!

First, don't get too concerned about this sort of thing. This style of interviewing is becoming more and more rare. The aim was to put the candidate under pressure and see how they responded. Even if you were ultimately offered the job, would you take it? Could you work for someone who behaved like that? Are you confident enough to deal with a situation like this, or could it upset you, or even permanently reduce your self-confidence? This type of interview also said a lot about the likely management style within the company! Don't take such comments to heart. Hostile interviewers do exist, so you need to prepare in case you do have the misfortune to come across one.

The facts and some reasons

Secondly, let's remember the facts. *They* chose to interview *you*. Nobody put a gun to their head! Therefore it follows logically that you have something they are interested in. So why on earth do some interviewers behave in a hostile manner?

To put you under pressure

This was the case in the above example. The interviewer wanted to make sure that any candidate hired would have the ability to stand up for themselves and the company under pressure and/or stress. It would have been a very stressful job, so perhaps the point needed to be assessed, but there was a better way in which this could have been done. This technique is often called the 'stress interview'.

Nervousness

Some interviewers are so nervous that they're slightly afraid of candidates. So they are a little aggressive to keep themselves in control of the situation – to show you who's boss. It's basically insecurity, so not something to worry about too much. If an interviewer is nervous of you, they must think you're a good candidate!

Testing determination

Some interviewers want to reassure themselves that you do really want the job. So they try to put you off a little, to see if you will get put off or whether you'll stay interested. It's 'prove you want the job' mentality, and really just testing your intentions and enthusiasm.

Genuine reaction testing

In some roles you will be dealing with the public, irate customers etc. So sometimes interviewers will be a little hostile with good reason – to assess how you react. They need to reassure themselves that you won't get defensive, or get aggressive back, especially if you will be dealing with difficult customers.

Bad interviewing

Let's face it, unfortunately there are just some bad interviewers out there – untrained, overzealous, pressurised people trying to do an interview without the relevant skills.

You just need to remember that none of this is about *you*, it's always about *them*, so don't let it get to you.

Never

◆ Turn the tables. Being hostile back rarely works.

◆ Try to rise above it by being clever. Being cleverer than the interviewer will probably threaten them, and they may get more hostile and difficult. It doesn't make you appear intelligent and capable, it often only makes you seem arrogant and a know-all.

HANDLING POOR QUESTIONS AND INTERVIEWERS

The poor interviewer

◆ Remember, employer interviews are rarely conducted by interviewing experts.

◆ Some interviewers may never have been trained to interview.

◆ They may be as nervous as you – or even more.

◆ If an interviewer is very nervous, try asking them a question to show interest and encourage them to relax.

◆ If they ask confusing or unclear questions, don't be afraid to ask them what they mean. You can't answer a question unless you understand it!

The pointless interview

If interviewers comment that they don't know why they are interviewing you, it's very frustrating. You have prepared to be interviewed for a vacancy, now it seems as if the interviewer doesn't even know if the vacancy exists. This is a horrid situation – it's tempting to think 'what's the point', but thinking like this will only make you give a very unenthusiastic performance.

First, the interviewer may be uninformed. They may be standing in for someone else, or even interviewing as part of a process. Just because they don't understand it, it doesn't mean there is no vacancy.

Secondly, this is really a chance to shine. You have a person within the company here in front of you and who knows, if they like you, they may know of something else you might be a good match for. Thinking like this keeps you enthusiastic and motivated.

If all else fails, chalk it up to experience and face it as a learning experience. Use the opportunity to polish your interview technique.

HANDLING THE DELICATE SUBJECT OF MONEY

Candidates are very often asked for information about their current salary. There are some golden rules that can help you out here – it is rarely in your best interests to give such information if you can possibly avoid it.

Only negotiate with people who have the authority to negotiate

The person who is interviewing you often does not have the authority to negotiate your salary or compensation. This will be particularly true in initial interviews, where the interviewer is acting as a screener to the next level. If you are asked at this stage what your salary requirements are, they are probably trying to decide whether or not to pass you forward for a second interview. So being evasive may not help.

Be vague

A good response is, 'I really like the job you've described, so I will consider any reasonable offer.' *Never* give a monetary figure if at all possible.

If under pressure

If you feel under pressure to give a salary expectation, always give them a range. The lower number should never be below what you require (your minimum requirement), or below the price advertised for the job if there has been one. Your upper number should be a reasonable amount higher than your lower one, and if you know the salary or range for the job, approximately ten per cent higher than that. So if a job advertisement states £25,000–27,000, and you need to earn at least £24,000, say £25–27,500.

For further advice see Chapter 8, Interviews and Meetings, to Discuss Offers.

WHAT HAPPENS NOW?

The process after this interview varies, depending on the role, the company and their recruitment processes. You are now dealing with the company or organisation itself, and they often have a defined recruitment process to follow. You may find yourself being interviewed by another person, perhaps someone more senior like a manager or head of the department. You may also find another interview is necessary with personnel or human resources.

Basically, more interviews are good news. It shows that you are progressing through the recruitment process of that company without being ruled out for the job. Candidates sometimes complain about having to go to several interviews at a company before they can make a decision. Of course this can be frustrating, but the more people you see the more chance you have of getting the job.

On the other hand, the more people you see the better chance you have of getting *another* job within the company, if you aren't chosen for the one you were interviewed for. If you don't get the job they may still have a suitable role in another department, or another role may come up soon.

More than one interview

A very rough rule of thumb is that it's rare to be offered a job after only one interview at a company. Larger companies tend to also require an interview with personnel or human resources. Complex roles may also involve meetings, interviews or discussions with others you will be working with, or managers of teams you will be dealing with regularly.

CHECKLIST

◆ Do remember that employers are interviewing you because they are interested in you working for them. So there is no need to be put off or intimidated by them – you must have something they want, or they wouldn't have asked to see you.

◆ Do prepare and make the right impression.

◆ Address their main concerns: Do you want the job? Would you fit in? Would you stay? Even if they don't ask these directly, remember to reassure them regarding these points.

◆ Ask sensible questions. This can be a real opportunity to add some facts or attention to an area of your skills or experience that you wish to highlight.

◆ Try to speak in terms that force the interviewer to imagine you actually doing the job. This always helps them to see you as potentially suitable and reassures them that you would fit in.

◆ Don't let hostile interviews throw you and shake your confidence. Even in the very worst case, they are an opportunity to practise your interview skills.

5

Personnel/HR and Senior Management Interviews

THE PURPOSE OF THE INTERVIEWS

Personnel/HR interviews

Personnel or human resources interviews (whichever name the company uses) can be a little hard to predict. In some companies they interview candidates first. In others they interview towards the end of the recruitment process. In others they don't interview at all – you may not even meet them until you join the company. Whenever in the process you face personnel or HR, there are some common things it can be useful to know.

Personnel or HR interviews at the beginning
When Personnel or HR interviews are at the beginning of the recruitment process, before you have seen a line manager, they are screening applicants. They may well be seeing large numbers of applicants, and will then pass a shortlist to the line manager(s) for them to decide who to interview. This is often because managers are busy doing

their own jobs, without the added workload of screening interviews with large numbers of candidates.

Personnel or HR would usually interview first where there are large numbers of vacancies as well, such as with graduate recruitment, or recruitment of large numbers of school leavers.

Sometimes it is just the company's process. For example, some companies prefer just personnel or HR to interview first – perhaps because they are trained to interview, and are therefore best able to give a good impression at interview to all applicants and prospective employees.

Personnel or HR interviews at the end
When personnel or HR interviews are near the end of the recruitment process, they often fulfil a slightly different function. Here they are usually given responsibility to negotiate salaries, or to question you about any doubts or concerns the line manager may have. By getting this far you know you have come through previous interviews and that the company is still interested in you. This is just one more interview stage.

The purpose of personnel/HR interviews
It's hard to generalise, but usually personnel or human resources people are just that. They're specialists in personnel or human resources – maybe even recruitment. So unless you are applying for a job in that area, they aren't likely to be asking you too many technical questions – that's the line manager's job. The emphasis of this interview is likely to be far more about:

◆ salary and benefits

◆ your reason for leaving

◆ your reasons for applying

◆ your motivation – what makes you tick at work

◆ your long-term career aspirations

◆ your general 'fit' for the company.

You might well be asked questions regarding:

◆ your communication skills

◆ time management

◆ your ability and experience of working in a team

◆ evidence of your self-motivation

◆ high standards of achievement from your past.

You could therefore prepare a little, by thinking of examples you could quote surrounding all these areas.

Senior management interviews

Very often, candidates find themselves faced with just one final hurdle – the senior management interview. The more senior you are, the more likely you are to have to meet with one or two final people. Why? There are many potential reasons, including:

◆ The job is a particularly influential one.

◆ The job is crucial to the business.

◆ They have had personality clashes in the past with employees doing that role or a similar one.

◆ You may be dealing with them on a regular basis.

◆ The job may involve a lot of external contact, so image is important.

◆ It may be that they just like to see everyone who is hired.

◆ Company policy is that everyone over a certain level is seen by 'the big boss'.

Relax!

If you have made it this far you are probably now the only candidate in the running! Relax, because you are now very likely to be offered the job. To make these meetings less formal and less daunting, and also to enable them to fit better into the schedule of senior people more easily, they can sometimes not be a formal interview. Lunch is common, or a drink in the early evening, or even dinner. This can make it easier to relax and be yourself, but beware, you are still probably being assessed.

THE BALANCE OF POWER

Personnel/HR interviews

Where Personnel or HR interviews come at the beginning of the recruitment process, you have very little power. They are probably dealing with large numbers of candidates for the job(s), and you are likely to be one of many.

On the other hand, where they interview towards the end of the recruitment process you are in a position of rather more power. Once you have come this far you know that the company is interested in you. They have often invested quite considerable time and effort in interviewing you. Plus time has been passing as the recruitment process went on, so their need for someone to do the job is getting ever more urgent. At this stage, if you are still in the running you must be in with a good chance.

So you may be in quite a good situation. But the job isn't yours just yet! The personnel or HR interview can be tricky, as you need to remember that these are the people in a company who should be the most highly trained to interview people. Therefore they are the most likely to spot any problem areas in your CV, or any answers you give that aren't what they are looking for.

Senior management interviews

In this situation there is power on both sides. The interviewer has power because they are senior management, and can almost certainly block your recruitment if they decide to for whatever reason. However, you also have power, because you are very likely to be the only candidate at this stage. Thus you are unlikely to be compared with others, just assessed and evaluated on your own merits.

MAKING THE RIGHT IMPRESSION

At this stage it is likely that someone has decided that you have the skills and abilities they need. Therefore the interview is more likely to be about 'fit'. Be prepared. Remember the comments and questions in the last chapter – use examples that are directly relevant wherever possible. Ask questions that force the interviewer to imagine you actually working there.

Salary and benefits

You should at all costs avoid salary discussions until they are making you a firm job offer, if possible. But with senior management or personnel/HR interviews, if they ask, you need to be prepared. After all, in many organisations this may be the final interview.

Know your current situation

Be thoroughly prepared to handle any unexpected discussions on salary and benefits. You can prepare by knowing the details of your current salary and benefits. Vague answers such as, 'I think it's £24,000, or maybe £25,000' will do you no favours. Neither will be being vague – saying 'about £25,000', when you're actually on £24,000! Know how much you earn, for goodness sake – as an annual salary, and also as an hourly rate if you are paid by the hour.

Current vs expected salary

In an ideal world, you should avoid disclosing your salary for as long as possible. But once you are dealing with personnel, HR or senior management, you may well be asked to. That's fine.

However, do try at all costs to avoid discussions about what salary you would *like* until you know they want to hire you. There are a number of reasons for this, and the subject of negotiating salary is dealt with in depth in Chapter 8, Interviews and Meetings to Discuss Offers.

Check your benefits
Now is the time to check what benefits you currently receive. Do you know how much pension your current employer provides? What about life insurance? Check your existing contract, and if in doubt ask a colleague, or if necessary personnel or human resources. There's nothing wrong with asking; people often assume you're checking before taking out a new policy. Make a list of benefits to refer to in the interview if necessary, in case you forget.

Establish what you want
Finally, research what the job is paying, and what you can afford to accept. You need to know what your bottom line is. If the job advert said £24–28,000, what *exactly* does that mean? It means they'll pay between £24,000 and £28,000. You might assume if you currently earn £24,000 that they wouldn't offer you anything less than, say, £26,000. I mean, everybody knows you normally increase your salary when changing jobs, right? *Wrong!*

Look at things from the employer's point of view. They may well be working within a set budget, and perhaps that company has set pay scales for this type of work. Or they may have other employees earning a certain salary, and to be fair to them they simply don't want to recruit anyone on a higher salary. There is far more going on with the employer's deliberations than a common convention that you increase your salary when you move jobs!

Senior management interviews

So how exactly do you make the right impression? There are a number of pointers that can help.

Remember their status

Senior management have usually gained their roles by a combination of years of experience and ability. They will usually be powerful individuals in the company, and whatever you think of them as individuals, their jobs demand respect. Always remember who they are, and don't get lulled into a false sense of security so that you lapse into over-familiarity, being too informal.

Stay confident

Having said that, stay confident. Don't be too much in awe of them, and therefore end up appearing shy and nervous. You want to appear confident and self-assured, whilst still respecting them. By being friendly and open you will appear to be at ease.

Help them imagine you as a colleague

In previous chapters we have advocated using examples, question responses and questions that force the interviewer to imagine you actually working for (and with) them. This is still a good idea, but don't overplay your hand. Appearing too sure of yourself can be irritating to some people, so it can be best to remember to use language like, '*if* I join you I'd like to start looking at . . . ,' and not '*when* I join you . . .' This allows you to make them imagine you working for them, without being presumptous.

QUESTIONS TO ASK

Remember, it is good practice to always ask one or two questions – it shows interest and enthusiasm for the job – provided of course that you don't ask questions that indicate otherwise! Personnel or HR look after the company policies and procedures, so it is useful to ask questions about these, if they haven't already been covered. With senior management you may even find that the conversation flags unless you have some questions. They may be relying on you to take part of the initiative. Here are some suggestions.

How does the company measure and review performance?

It's useful to know whether they operate an appraisal scheme or some form of performance management. Is there a link to pay reviews, salary increases and/or bonuses or performance related pay (PRP)?

How long do people usually stay with the company?

Do they have a large population of people who don't stay very long? If you want a role that you can grow and stay in for several years, do you want to join a company where most people leave after 18 months?

Why did the last person leave?

You may not get the real answer, but it's a good question. Were they promoted? If so, this shows that you can progress within the company. If you're told that they left to go and work somewhere else, it's very hard to find a way of asking why politely, but it would be very useful to know. Depending on how things are going and how much rapport you have with the interviewer, you could possibly ask, 'do you mind if I ask whether you know why?'

Why they left can give you a very good idea of whether or not you want the job, if you have any doubts. It can make the difference between deciding to take it and waiting for something more right for you. For example, if you are a little concerned that the job isn't very challenging, and the previous person left to gain a role with more responsibility outside the company, it could mean they had to leave as there were no internal prospects. You might need to be prepared to stay in that role for a while, and is that really what you want?

Where does this position and department fit into the company?

If you have any doubts about this, now is the time to ask!

What would you say is the management style of the section or department?

This is especially useful if you aren't sure whether or not you would work well with the manager/supervisor you have met. Think about it – if you have found the person who would be your manager a little intimidating, and you were told the style was 'quite disciplined and structured – formal really' wouldn't that tell you something? Also, if you had found the person very informal and surprisingly easy-going, wouldn't it be reassuring to be told the style was, very relaxed and friendly, but managed well. Everyone is given responsibility for their own work, and access to the manager when they need it?

Can you explain the structure of the department to me?

Obviously only use this if it hasn't been explained in detail. Or modify the question, and ask them to explain the overall structure of the company.

How many employees are there in the department? And in the rest of the company?

You don't necessarily need to know this, but it makes conversation and shows interest in the company as a whole.

Are there any significant changes in the department coming up?

This is helpful information to find out, as well as showing how interested you are.

How do you rate yourselves against your competition?

This is a question that requires them to think. It also enables you to sell your own application, by going on to say how you view the competition as well.

POTENTIAL PITFALLS

Personnel/HR interviews

The personnel or HR interview is quite an important one. This is because the personnel or HR interviewer you face will probably have been extensively trained in interviewing. Other interviewers may have been on a course, or have been trained in some way, but rarely will they have had the same level of training, or the same experience at interviews. Therefore, although some people take this interview less seriously than others where they may be asked more technical questions, you are probably facing your most skilled interviewer.

This isn't something to worry about unnecessarily, just be aware of it. If you aren't sure what they are asking, clarify what they want before responding. Glib, superficial answers aren't likely to do you any favours – be prepared to think through your answers and be honest. There is nothing wrong with saying, 'Can I have a second to think about that?'

Senior management interviews

This is the opposite situation! Senior managers may have been trained in interviewing, but it could have been some time ago and they may not have had any recent training. Also, in view of their position, they may do very few interviews. Thus they can often be awkward interviewers, not quite sure what to say to you.

Be very careful of alcohol!

If the meeting takes place over a drink or meal, it can often mean alcohol being offered. Unless you really don't drink, don't refuse, as it can be awkward to explain. By the same token, don't have more than one or two glasses of wine.

Sometimes senior management use these meetings to try to have an enjoyable time, and get you to relax with some drinks, and then see how you bear up under questions once you're had your tongue loosened! Alcohol lowers inhibitions, remember, so you are far more likely to make a slip and say something you otherwise wouldn't if you have had a few drinks. A couple of glasses of wine will ensure you don't appear unsociable, but that you treat the meeting seriously. Standing firm under pressure to drink more can be a test in itself . . .

WHAT HAPPENS NOW?

A decision will usually be forthcoming after this interview. After a personnel or HR interview you may be asked to meet with a senior manager – but once this is done you are usually waiting for a decision now. It makes sense to ask what the process is following the interview. If you are told that someone will get back to you, there is nothing wrong with asking *roughly* when you might hear. Being too specific just sounds fussy and even a little desperate, so make sure you ask casually and don't be pushy.

CHECKLIST

◆ Always remember that the emphasis of the interview may be on non-technical questions.

◆ Be aware that if you have made it this far, you have a good chance.

◆ Prepare thoroughly. Just because it is a personnel or HR interview doesn't mean you shouldn't have your facts and figures ready.

◆ Prepare some questions to ask, to show your interest and to make conversation if necessary.

◆ Prepare to be interviewed both by a skilled interviewer, or someone with rusty interviewing skills. Both need careful handling.

◆ Don't be afraid to ask when you might hear.

6

Assessment Centres

WHAT ARE ASSESSMENT CENTRES?

The term assessment centre is not about a place; it is used to describe a selection process. Assessment centres combine interviews with a range of other assessment activities. This enables employers to gain a more rounded picture of you when making recruitment decisions. They can involve a large investment on the part of the employer, in both time and money.

Traditional recruitment interviews often focus on past performance: how well you can discuss and explain situations you have previously dealt with. Assessment centres, on the other hand, simulate the competencies required for the job, and are looking at how well you might be able to perform if selected.

When are you likely to face assessment centres?

Many employers have assessment centres as part of their recruitment process. Traditionally they take place after initial screening interviews, but can be used at any stage. They are often used when there are large numbers of people to be assessed, for example with graduate recruitment programmes or training schemes. Assessment centres are also more popular with public sector employers. You usually find assessment centres where the organisation is looking for more than one candidate.

The history of assessment centres

Assessment centres are not new inventions. In fact they were developed by the War Office during the Second World War to select candidates to become Officers for the Armed Forces. The War Office Selection Boards (WOSBies) were devised as they wanted to assess candidates in a range of scenarios that simulated 'real-life' situations.

What happens in a typical assessment centre?

Typically you will join a group of other candidates for a series of tests or 'assessments'. These are designed to show your potential employer(s) whether or not you can demonstrate most of the personal and technical skills required or preferred to do the job. Assessment centre programmes can be intensive, and may involve at least a whole day, so be prepared to eat lunch and possibly other meals there. You might even be required to stay overnight for a two-day assessment centre.

You will usually be assessed against a set of key requirements, or competencies, which the employer is looking for. There are many tasks which employers use at assessment centres. They include group exercises and individual exercises. Because there are several activities, it does mean that just because you feel you have performed badly in one, you can still retrieve the situation in other exercises or activities. This chapter outlines common activities you may face at an assessment centre.

What are they assessing?

There is no set list. Typical qualities, skills, attitudes or competencies an employer might be looking for could include the following, but this is by no means an exhaustive list, or a list that every employer might be looking for *all* of!

◆ analytical ability

◆ calmness

◆ commercial awareness

◆ decision-making

◆ drive

◆ flexibility

◆ interpersonal skills

◆ leadership

◆ logical thinking

◆ motivation

◆ negotiating and persuasion skills

◆ planning

◆ presentation skills

◆ response to pressure

◆ self-confidence

◆ strategic thinking

- teamwork

- verbal communication.

Why have assessment centres?

Advantages for you

- You often get to find out a lot more about the company.

- You get to understand the organisation's expectations and values.

- Successful candidates can often find they have met many staff, and feel more 'at home' and part of the company.

- As well as tests, you often have access to staff and managers from the company on an informal basis, such as over meals, coffee etc.

Advantages for the company

- They can make better decisions. The idea is that the more data you have about a candidate, the more likely you are to be able to make the right recruitment decision – the reliability and validity of selection decisions is improved. There is a large body of evidence that assessment centres which are well designed and run are one of the most valid methods for predicting a candidate's performance in a job. The evidence also shows that they are one of the fairest and most objective means of gathering data to make recruitment decisions.

- Ease of planning and administration. If you are recruiting large numbers of candidates, juggling interviewing schedules can be an absolute nightmare, so many companies prefer to have a day or few days of assessment centres and see all the candidates over a short period of time. This would apply, as we have already said, for recruitment such as graduate recruitment, training scheme intakes etc.

◆ Increasing management and/or staff involvement. One big advantage of assessment centres is that existing managers and/or supervisors become more involved in the recruitment and selection of new employees. Obviously they need to be trained for this, but it does mean that they can participate more than usual. Many managers can be involved in assessment centres, but the number of people who can interview each candidate is limited by practicality. The fact that there are social elements to an assessment centre, such as tea, coffee, lunch etc, means that a larger number of staff can get to meet candidates.

The other applicants

Be nice to everyone!
Always be courteous and pleasant to other candidates. Your prospective employer may well judge how you will behave with your colleagues by how you behave with other candidates during the selection process. It's surprising how much skilled recruiters can pick up on, so don't fall into the trap of letting other candidates make you appear anything other than positive and professional.

It's not necessarily a competition
It is highly likely that more than one candidate will be selected from those attending the assessment centre. So you

should not feel that you are in competition with the other candidates in any way. In fact, one or more of them could well end up being your colleagues, if you get the job, so co-operation and friendliness is in order. Bearing in mind that one of the big things likely to be assessed is co-operation and teamwork, you cannot afford to treat an assessment centre like a competition.

Handling difficult candidates

Some of the other applicants may be less friendly to you. They may regard you as a rival, and treat you accordingly. This can make exercises difficult, as teamwork is often essential to succeed. Take it as a compliment that they think you are strong competition and rise above it all! You can only look better by comparison.

Be conscious of social settings

As well as the interviews, exercises and tests, the programme of an assessment centre also has an informal or 'social' side. How you mix and who with is something that may increase (or decrease) your chances of being successful. Managers, staff and candidates meet each other over an extended period, so candidates can often be observed interacting with other candidates in other ways:

◆ over dinner

◆ in conversations at the bar

◆ when touring the building.

THE EXERCISES

Group exercises

Why have group exercises?
These are simply designed to see how you work in a group:

◆ Are you a leader or follower?

◆ Do you communicate well, or hang back and let everyone else get on with it?

◆ Do you argue when challenged, or stay calm and polite?

◆ There may also be an element of comparing you with other group members.

What do they involve?
Group exercises can include candidates being required to discuss a topic or resolve a problem. Such exercises are typically designed to examine areas such as planning, organising, leadership, communication skills, analysis, synthesis, influencing etc. They can also be practical exercises, like building a simple tower or bridge from building blocks and materials under certain conditions and restrictions, such as not being able to step on certain parts of the floor etc.

Interacting with others
In a group exercise you are, to a certain extent, dependent on the other people in your group. Difficult personalities may make it very hard for you to behave normally, but remember, in group exercises usually *how* you do something is far more important to the assessor than *what* you do.

Conflict situations

You need to be aware that some exercises are deliberately set up to induce a conflict between group members. If this happens, stay calm and assertive. Be flexible, to accommodate others, without compromising your own situation. Never criticise others unless the remark is constructive. Above all else, always try to reach a group conclusion or decision, even if this cannot be unanimous.

Individual exercises

What are individual exercises?

These are exercises designed to assess your own individual ability. Sometimes you may be in a room with a group of people, but all given individual exercises to do separately. It's important to remember that this is an individual exercise, and so there is no point in being intimidated or put off by others who work more quickly or in a different way from you. After all they may be totally wrong, so there is no point in being conscious of what others are doing really.

What do they involve?

Exercises can range from writing an essay on a topic to solving a problem. Interviews are the most common form of individual exercise, when you think about it, and a 'traditional' one-to-one interview may occur, or you may face a 'panel interview' with several interviewers. This may take place instead of a one-to-one interview, or as well, so be prepared.

Specific exercises

The rest of this chapter will concentrate on specific exercises you may face, whether they are conducted in a group or individually. For example, a case study might be carried out individually, or in a group.

CASE STUDIES

What are case studies?

One particular type of exercise is a case study. This is where you are given a business scenario, and you have to analyse it and complete a task. This may typically be to make decisions about what should be done, to prepare a presentation of your ideas, or to write a report. This is usually an individual exercise, but may also be carried out as a group exercise where it would allow the employer to assess your discussion and communication skills, as well as your ability to solve the case study.

Handling the information

Typically you would be provided with a large amount of factual information in the scenario or as additional information.

Handling irrelevant information

Not all of the information given to you may be relevant, as part of the assessment may be to see how good you are at managing large volumes of information.

Handling ambiguous information
You may also find that some of the information is ambiguous, so beware of jumping to too large conclusions. If you have to make an assumption, say where you have done so.

Handling contradictory information
Another potential problem is that some of the information given may even be contradictory. If this is the case you may either have to make an assumption, as above, or allow for possibilities in your answer ('if X is true, then I recommend . . . If, however, Y is true, then my recommendation would change to . . .').

Useful advice for case studies

There are some points that can help you manage a case study:

◆ Keep to the time allowed – don't lose track of time and not get the work done.

◆ Answer the question or task you are set – if you are asked to prepare a report, prepare a report. If asked to produce a presentation, do a presentation, not a report!

◆ Explain your thinking. If you have made an assumption or judgement about data that is wrong, this can be offset if you have explained that this is what you did. Otherwise, there is no explanation for what could be a totally wrong answer.

◆ If you are asked to make a decision, make one – don't sit on the fence. If your decision is dependent on assumptions or other data, say so. ('In the absence of other data, I recommend . . . However, in the real world I would first like to check the figures for . . . before making any decisions.')

◆ Don't panic. The exercise may have been set up so that you cannot finish. Just do the best you can in the time allocated.

HANDLING PANEL INTERVIEWS

What are panel interviews?

A panel interview is where you are intervicwed by more than one person. This can be very stressful, especially if you're not expecting it. One interviewer is nerve-wracking enough for some people, two is added pressure, three or more is very daunting even at the best of times.

You need to remember that, very often, panel interviews are not as planned and efficiently organised as you might think. It's tempting to imagine that the interviewers have a well-thought-out schedule of who will ask what questions and when. In real life not only is this not very common, but human nature being what it is, people will jump in and ask a question when they feel the time is right – perhaps when you say something that makes them interested or curious.

Who to address your answers to

People can only answer one question at a time. When someone asks you a question, look at them and answer them. It's *their* question. But don't exclude the other interviewers. As you are answering, focus on the person who asked you the question, but look round at the other interviewers as you are talking. It's that simple – you don't have to do anything that you wouldn't do at a party or meal with friends!

You may find that one person doesn't ask any questions. They may be taking notes, or they may just not ask anything. Don't ignore them just because they aren't asking anything. You need to give eye contact and attention to everyone.

Find potential 'allies'

Your potential boss
If the person who would be your potential boss if you got the job is on the panel, make sure you give them plenty of attention. Don't ignore others, but remember that your manager may well have a casting vote, and will certainly be important to have on your side. In any event, the most successful candidate may not get hired if the manager doesn't feel they could work with them.

People who are supportive
Look for someone on the panel who seems to be friendly, or agreeing with what you are saying. They are an ally, and you can look to them for support and encouragement. But don't be tempted to end up speaking mainly to them just because they are listening sympathetically and encouragingly – you need to make an impression on everyone, remember.

Find the ringleader if there is one
There is often one person leading the panel, or someone who naturally takes over and to whom the others defer. If you

can spot this, make sure you try to impress him or her, as they may well influence the opinions of others later, when they discuss how the interview went.

Handling interruptions and several questions at once

Handling interruptions
If you are interrupted, it doesn't matter who does the interrupting – whether or not it was their question. Just answer and deal with the interruption, focusing on the person who raised it. If it helps, pretend there is only one interviewer.

Dealing with multiple questions
If there is a pause in the questions, or two people start to ask a question at once, this is nothing to worry about. It's their problem and lack of co-ordination – let them sort it out! If you are really in doubt, just ask, 'Sorry, what would you like me to answer first?' Disorganised panel interviews are not your fault, and there's no point getting upset or distracted by multiple interviewers.

SIMULATIONS

What are simulations?
Simulations are exercises where you resolve a problem that is an example of a real-life situation. They range from a group of candidates playing roles in an exercise (for example playing members in a meeting, to assess teamwork and/or communication), to individually doing a case study.

These exercises are quite good, because they can be fun, and they give you a real feel for the work you might be doing if you got the job. Designed well they are also quite fair tests, as they are based on how you might perform in the job, not what you have done before. A simulation might be a group exercise such as described earlier, where you have to construct a bridge from blocks and rope without stepping on certain areas of the floor.

Key competencies
The employer is looking for evidence that you are reasonably sensible, have common sense and can solve problems. They need to know you can react sensibly to tasks, and have ideas about how to create solutions. They are usually not looking for lengthy analysis in depth, just an indication that you can cope with the demands of the job.

The 'in-tray' exercise
A common simulation exercise is an 'in-tray exercise'. This is where the contents of an imaginary in-tray are presented to you to prioritise and/or deal with. This can be a very useful exercise, if it is designed so that the in-tray contents are typical things that the jobholder might face – for example samples from an actual task or good quality examples. The exercise requires you to read the items, sort them, analyse the contents, assign priorities and sometimes go on to regenerate responses. Other exercises might include planning an event, evaluating a case study etc.

DISCUSSIONS

What are discussion exercises?

These are discussions on a set topic. You may be given a role, or a leader for the discussion, but this is rare. Usually the group is simply set a topic which you are asked to discuss for a fixed amount of time. The topic is usually a controversial one, in order to stimulate lots of discussion!

Key competencies

Obviously, it is your communications skills that are being tested here. Extremes of behaviour such as saying nothing or dominating the discussion will probably not be looked on favourably. Generally speaking, employers will be looking for evidence of:

◆ participation and contribution

◆ reasoning with and convincing others

◆ effective communication

◆ listening skills

◆ negotiation and co-operation

◆ interaction with others etc.

Advice for discussions

◆ Do not clam up and say nothing.

◆ Don't talk too much.

◆ Consider both *what* you say and *how* you say it –

don't antagonise people or be too abrupt if you need to contradict them.

◆ Don't respond in kind to antagonism from others.

◆ Don't be afraid to bring in any outside knowledge you have – the brief may not be complete, and sometimes you may have to bring in other facts.

◆ Don't make up outrageous facts just because you may be role playing! Candidates sometimes do this, and it may be fun, but it can also detract from the good qualities they are showing.

EXERCISES IN GROUPS

The exercises
Basically, these exercises are designed to see how well you perform in a team or group. A typical exercise might be being given a task to solve. Remember that group dynamics are important here – the employer is probably looking for people who have ideas, and can convince and persuade others.

Key competencies
The employer is most likely to be looking for people who can work easily with others – good team players. Therefore extremes, such as saying little or nothing, or hogging the limelight, can count against you. Whether the exercises are physical or mental, the employers are looking for the same things:

- teamwork

- participation and contribution

- reasoning with and convincing others

- effective communication

- listening skills

- negotiation and co-operation

- interaction with others

- possibly leadership ability

- ability to cope with difficult people

- coping under pressure.

Types of group exercise

Leaderless exercises
These are exercises where everyone has the same brief and the common objective of achieving some sort of task. No leader is nominated, and employers often look to see who naturally emerges as group leader, or who decisively takes control of the situation. Many candidates therefore assume that they have to try to become the leader in order to shine during the exercise. Remember, the leader isn't always successful, so don't rush in – you can make just as good an impression without being leader!

In fact, many employers will have seen whole exercises struggle because two or more people spent the beginning of the exercise fighting for leadership of the group. The rest of the time is often insufficient to achieve the task, which demotivates everyone. Far from giving a good image of the leader who 'wins', they are actually quite unlikely to get hired!

Assigned role exercises

This is an exercise where everyone has an assigned role that they must carry out. This may be as simple as assigning a leader and one or two other key roles, or it can extend into everyone having a different brief. This can often (and deliberately) cause conflict, and candidates are then assessed on how well they handle that situation and the resulting conflict.

General advice for tasks or exercises in groups

◆ Make sure you understand the task.

◆ Don't waste time (or let the group waste time) on details once you understand the task properly.

◆ Decide on priorities – make sure everyone knows what they are.

◆ Be assertive with others, and make your point, but compromise where necessary.

◆ Work with the others, not on your own.

◆ Make contributions to the group, and recognise and encourage contributions from others in the group.

◆ Don't lose your temper or become irritated with people.

◆ Keep your sense of humour, but don't trivialise the task or anyone's actions or contributions.

◆ Keep an eye on the time – most tasks are set against a tight time limit and people can often forget this. Some-one usually needs to remind people how much time they have left.

GIVING A PRESENTATION

The exercise

One frequent exercise at an assessment centre is giving a presentation. This may be either on a topic of your choice, or on a topic you are given. Sometimes you are asked to prepare a short presentation and bring it with you to present – this saves time on the day.

If you are given a topic to present, this can sometimes be in the form of a mass of data to analyse and present. Do not get overwhelmed by this – structure and content are important. Boil the facts down to key items you can present clearly and simply. Don't get too complex.

You may have to present to just two or three members of staff, to a larger group, or to the group of candidates at the assessment centre.

Key competencies

The employer is looking to see how well you can put a point across. They are testing your ability to prepare and com-municate. They are likely to be unimpressed by people who are excessively nervous, and cannot speak to a group, as this wouldn't be one of the exercises if it wasn't required for the job.

Helpful advice for presentations

◆ How you present yourself will be crucial.

◆ Introduce yourself and your subject clearly.

◆ Be enthusiastic and be interested in your subject – it's infectious and will usually make your audience interested.

◆ Make eye contact with the audience. If there are several people, move your gaze around, making eye contact with them in turn.

◆ Speak clearly and at a sensible speed.

◆ Speak to the audience, not at the floor, the back of the room, your notes or a projector.

◆ Practise beforehand if at all possible, making sure you stick to the time limit allowed.

◆ Practise with any equipment or visual aids you will be using.

◆ Try to keep things structured logically.

◆ Summarise at the end.

◆ Stick to the time limit. It is embarrassing and makes things very difficult if you run over time – the employers may penalise you, and your audience is likely to get uncomfortable and embarrassed, which can damage your confidence for other exercises.

PSYCHOMETRIC TESTS

Assessment centres may include a psychometric test. These tests may also be carried out separately from an assessment centre – it just depends on the employer. Psychometric tests will be discussed in full in the next chapter.

CHECKLIST

◆ Understand the assessment function of assessment centres and maintain your conduct accordingly. Even in social or informal situations you may be being assessed.

◆ Remember, it's not a competition, and approaching an assessment centre from that perspective may actually reduce your chances.

◆ Do not try to take leadership during an exercise for the sake of it. If you feel you are the best person to lead, that's one thing. But the myth that being the leader gets you hired can make you appear domineering and aggressive.

◆ How you do things is usually more important than what you do.

◆ Understand how to handle each of the potential exercises, and practise if possible.

◆ Be aware of eye contact during panel interviews.

7

Psychometric Tests

TESTING – WHAT AND WHY?

When are psychometric tests used?

Psychometric tests may be used on their own, before or at the end of an interview, or at an assessment centre. They are simply a method used in addition to interviews, CVs and other assessment exercises, to gain additional supporting evidence that you have the required skills and abilities for the job in question. They attempt to measure whether or not you have the specific skills or the appropriate personal qualities required for that job.

A test is a way of assessing human behaviour, or certain aspects of it. It is likely that you will face testing at some stage of your career, so it is useful to be aware of testing.

What is a psychometric test?

The term psychometric test is commonly being used nowadays to refer to all types of testing. The British Psychological Society (BPS) has the following definition:

'Instruments designed to produce a quantitative assessment of some psychological attribute or attributes.'

'A psychological test is any procedure on the basis of which inferences are made concerning a person's capacity, propensity or liability to act, react, experience, or to structure or order thought or behaviour in particular ways.'

You will often find them called other names, such as:

◆ occupational tests

◆ psychological tests

◆ personality tests.

What are the rules about their usage – what rights do you have?

A great deal of research goes into such tests, to ensure that they are measuring what they set out to measure and to make certain that they are fair to those who sit them. The Chartered Institute of Personnel (CIPD) gives the following advice:

'Test administrators should ensure that individuals receive:

◆ Advance notice that they will be required to take tests.

◆ Notice of the duration of tests and whether this is significant in interpreting results.

◆ Adequate time to allow them to make any practical arrangements to allow them to take the tests.

◆ Access to an appropriate environment free from interference in which to take tests.

◆ Adequate information about the requirements of each test they are required to complete, and the opportunity to question any arrangements before taking the tests.

◆ Information on the arrangements for feedback.'

Although this is only advice, it is good advice. If you feel you have been tested in a way that is inappropriate or unprofessional, however, as a candidate you are unlikely to improve your chances of getting the job if you complain!

Types of test
There are two main types of test:

1. Tests to assess how well you perform – tests we shall call **aptitude tests** in this chapter, although they can cover far more.
2. Tests to assess why you perform or behave in the way you do. These are tests we shall call **personality tests** in this chapter, although again they can include far more sorts of tests than just personality.

Why test?
So why do employers use tests? You might be forgiven for thinking that, after three interviews, anyone should be able to make their minds up without any extra tricks! But remember, interviews aren't actually very objective. People do base judgements on first impressions, or personal likes and dislikes (subjectivity). Any interviewer, especially one who is inexperienced, may have a tendency without even realising it to recruit based on a first impression, or on

finding that they are interviewing someone whom they personally like. Interviewers may also suffer from 'stereotyping'.

An objective test such as a psychometric test will not make any allowances for these personal preferences to enter the decision-making process. Psychometric tests are objective, and their scoring is the same for everyone. Some researchers believe that tests are more than twice as effective as interviews in selecting the right applicant for a job.

Tests that are administered competently are good selection methods, but no selection method is perfect. These tests are designed so that every person who takes the test has exactly the same questions and an identical amount of time in which to answer them. The score each person gets is then converted, by comparing it to a representative sample of people who have taken the test. This will inform the tester whether you have scored below average, average, or above average, and by how much.

UNDERSTAND WHAT THEY ARE LOOKING FOR
Testing is carried out to compare you with the 'ideal employee'. The idea is that the employer has an idea of what competencies or abilities/qualities would enable someone to do well at the job. The test is to determine whether or not you have those competencies. This is important. It means that the employer is testing you compared with an 'ideal employee', not compared to perfect scores. Scoring as high as possible may not be what they are looking for.

For example, if an employer tested for analytical skills and flexibility, scoring very highly in both isn't necessarily the best idea. Their ideal employee might be someone who follows rules and processes and never deviates from them, so they could be looking for a high score in analytical skills and low flexibility. On the other hand, they might be looking for someone who is flexible and able to make quick decisions without detailed research, so they are looking for high flexibility but low analytical skills. Get the idea?

APTITUDE TESTS

What are aptitude tests?
As we said earlier, aptitude tests are tests to assess **how well** you perform. They are tests of:

◆ ability

◆ aptitude

◆ intelligence

◆ performance

◆ problem-solving

◆ skill

◆ specific skills, such as how to programme a computer

◆ verbal or numerical reasoning.

What do they measure?
These are tests that measure your **individual performance** as compared with a given standard, such as a representative

population average or 'norm'. The test results are then used, together with other information gleaned, to make a selection decision. It is worth bearing in mind that as aptitude testing is only part of the recruitment process, poor test performance may not necessarily mean you are not successful!

How do they work?

These tests generally require correct answers to questions. They are timed and administered under strict examination conditions and it is normal that the test is set so that you are unlikely to finish all the tasks within the given time limit. In many tests you may find that as you go through the test, the questions or tasks become more difficult so they take longer. Don't worry if you can't finish the test – this will be taken into account, as the test group you will be assessed against will have faced exactly the same tasks as you in the same time.

Ways of improving test scores

Here are some ways in which you could try to enhance your chances of doing well in tests. But please remember that tests are designed so that problems have to be solved from scratch, or so there is no right or wrong answer.

◆ Brush up on maths, such as fractions, percentages, averages, charts and tables. There are relatively common tests for numerical reasoning.

◆ Practise tests. This may not help you with the answers, but it could help you become familiar with the time pressure of a timed test, and test conditions. Remember that many tests are designed to be more than is achievable in the time allowed, so don't panic about having to finish the whole test.

◆ Try puzzle books such as logic puzzles if you might face a reasoning ability test.

◆ Search the Internet – there are a wealth of tests available online, some more reliable than others.

PERSONALITY TESTS

What are personality tests?

How successful you are likely to be in a job doesn't just depend on whether or not you can do it. It also depends on your personal qualities. Personality tests are tests to assess **why** you perform in that way. They are tests of:

◆ personality

◆ values

◆ interests

◆ motivation.

These tests are designed to give an insight into your preferred outlook, way of thinking and behavioural style. As such there are no hard and fast 'right answers', so these tests tend to actually be questionnaires and inventories rather than 'tests'. Often they are called inventories or questionnaires, but for ease of reference we will use the word test in this chapter.

What exactly do they measure?

Personality tests explore the way in which you do things, including why, and how you behave in certain circumstances. They explore your preferences and attitudes. They are designed to predict how those factors will affect the way you work. The tests are aimed at finding out about you as an individual, your style of working and the way you deal with situations, to predict how you might behave in the job. They are almost always paper and pencil exercises (although they are sometimes computer-based) and frequently have no set time limit. They are not tests as such, but carefully designed questionnaires that ask you to be honest about the way you would behave in particular circumstances.

What do the results mean?

Your results are usually called your 'profile'. In order to assess your results, this is compared with the results of a test group of others (a 'norm group') that have taken the test in the past. Because these tests attempt to characterise you as an individual, and due to the level of expertise required to interpret them, only individuals qualified by the British Psychological Society should administer them.

Advice for personality tests

◆ Be yourself! As there are usually no 'right' or 'wrong' answers you should just try to answer as honestly and naturally as possible. That will enable the profile produced of you to be as accurate it can be.

◆ Remember that if you are *not* honest, your profile may end up helping you get a job for which you are really not well suited!

◆ If in doubt, use the answer that feels most right to you – 'gut feeling'.

◆ Never try to give an answer just because it is what you think the employer might want you to say.

Tests of interest or motivation

These are mainly tests or measures of what things appeal to you and what things you find unappealing. The tests therefore have no 'correct' responses. 'Motivational measures' are aimed at understanding your interests in a general way, to show the kinds of activities and work in which you are likely to be comfortable. For example, if you are motivated by stimulation and learning new things, and the job requires someone who is a detail-conscious person, who is content to do repetitive work motivated by it being accurate, you and the job are not well matched.

QUESTIONS TO ASK

There are actually very few questions to ask at psychometric tests. They aren't like an interview in this respect. Here are some that you should feel comfortable asking, should you wish.

Can you explain that to me again please?

Never be afraid to ask for an explanation of the instructions if you aren't sure. Feeling silly for asking for additional explanation is far better than messing up the entire test because you haven't understood.

Will I have an opportunity to see my results?

Some companies let you see your results, or even take a copy home with you. Others never let you see them. If you would like to see them, feel free to ask – they can always say no!

Is it possible to have some feedback about the results afterwards?

This is subtly different from asking for an actual copy. You might like to have someone talk you through your results. Especially with personality tests, it can be very frustrating or even worrying to go away without knowing what the results were. If you then don't get the job, it can even make you wonder whether there was anything unusual in your result! Don't be afraid to ask for feedback. Most companies will give you brief feedback as to the results, but there is no guideline that says they must do this. If you have a burning desire to get the results of a personality test, try one of the ones freely available on the Internet (although be warned that some are better than others).

CAN YOU MANIPULATE A TEST?

Myths and legends

There are a lot of myths and stories about tests and how easy some of them are to manipulate. It is true that experienced individuals can slant answers towards a particular direction in a personality test. For example, it can be easy to see answers that would lead to a profile of someone who is bubbly, enthusiastic and extrovert. But how do you know what the employer is looking for? You could be biasing your test in totally the wrong direction if they are looking for a quiet, calm team player! Even if you could manipulate a test, it's not a good idea to try.

DEALING WITH TESTS

Before the test starts

◆ Stay calm. Panic won't help your performance.

◆ Sit comfortably. Don't worry about how you look whilst you are being tested. Feel free to loosen ties, remove jackets, roll up sleeves etc so you are comfortable to give your best performance without distractions.

◆ Ask questions if necessary – don't worry about looking stupid in front of other candidates – they aren't the ones you have to impress.

◆ Read and obey the instructions *exactly* – if it asks you to tick boxes, tick them, and don't shade them in and vice versa.

◆ Don't make assumptions – ask if you aren't sure about anything.

◆ If there are any sample or practice questions, use your opportunity to do them, to make sure you are doing them correctly.

During the test

◆ Work quickly but don't rush.

◆ Make sure you answer in the correct place on the answer sheet.

- Read questions thoroughly before trying to answer them.

- Don't agonise over a question you can't do, but move on to the next one.

- Don't waste time double-checking questions with easy or obvious answers unless you have spare time at the end.

- Check the time. It's easier to rush or work too slowly if you have no awareness of the time left. Check your own watch at the beginning of the test, so you know how much time is left at a glance.

- Don't try to do each question in the same time. Some tests are designed to start with easy questions, which get progressively more lengthy.

- Ignore other people. Just because they may be turning over pages more quickly, it doesn't mean they are getting the answers right!

- If you have time left at the end, go back and check your answers.

- Take some deep breaths occasionally and look up – it relieves the stress!

- If you can't answer, move on to another question and come back to the one you're stuck on.

- Forget about looking for easy or trick questions. Just work methodically through the test.

- At the end, return to any questions you got stuck on.

- It is usually better *not* to guess answers you aren't sure of unless instructed to do so. Some tests look at how many correct answers you got from the number you answered, so they measure percentage correct. Guessing may make you answer more questions, but with fewer correct answers.

Online practice sites

There are a number of Internet sites that have practice questions or tests that you can use freely. Here are some website addresses. Please note that these can only be correct at the time of printing, and websites may change their content.

http://www.morrisby.co.uk – click practice test from menu
http://www.kent.ac.uk/careers/psychtests.htm
http://www.shldirect.com
http://www.assessmentday.co.uk
http://www.kenexa.com/solu_practicetests.html
http://www.psychometric-success.com/
http://www.prospects.ac.uk/links/aptitudetests

WHAT HAPPENS NOW?

Always ask for feedback. Some people give feedback on the day, but it is surprising how many employers never offer feedback to individuals. It is both perfectly acceptable and a good idea to ask how you can obtain feedback at the session. There is nothing wrong with ringing up afterwards and asking for test feedback, especially if you didn't get the job – this can even be a better idea, as you may be less stressed a day or two after the test, and more likely to understand and take in the feedback.

Feedback can help you do better in other tests in the future. After you have received feedback, there is absolutely nothing wrong with asking a tester for advice on how to improve for next time.

If you disagree with the feedback, remember, this is what the test results say. Therefore *you* have given the tester this information. So if it's not accurate, you need to rethink how honest you were in the test. The exception to this is if you are offered feedback on the day. If the decision hasn't yet been made it is worth mentioning anything you disagree with to the tester. For example, if you assumed something, and that's why you answered in a particular way, let them know. It can sometimes make a difference.

CHECKLIST

◆ Understand the two main types of test.

◆ Never try to manipulate a test – you can't know exactly what they are looking for!

◆ You can practise for aptitude tests, to try to brush up your test skills.

◆ Don't attempt to be anything other than yourself in personality tests.

◆ Never be afraid to ask for explanation or clarification.

◆ Stay calm and work sensibly and methodically.

◆ Ask for feedback. It can be very helpful to know what the test results said about you.

8

Interviews and Meetings to Discuss Offers

COMPANY ATTITUDES TO SALARY NEGOTIATIONS

Salary negotiations can be a potential minefield. If you have been interviewed via an agency or head-hunter, this is where they take the stress out of job-hunting for you, as they should do the negotiating between you and the employer. But if not, you face this yourself. Candidates often feel concerns about pitching their requirements too high, and not getting the job, or selling themselves short and not being paid what they are worth or what might have been on offer. Let's start by taking a look at how companies view salary negotiations.

Job offers are not easy for companies to arrive at. In general, although there are many ways they arrive at a figure to offer you for a particular, these tend to fall into two broad categories, which we will call **competitive offers** and **opening offers**.

Competitive offers

A company making competitive offers analyses the employment market and what they already pay other employees doing similar work. They may find out what rival companies are paying, or benchmark their own salaries to the outside market. They might have a specialist in personnel or human resources who specialises in 'compensation and benefits'. When they arrive at an offer to make to a candidate, they attempt to be competitive.

How offers are arrived at
Offers are made based on the fact that they are:

◆ competitive

◆ fair salary or wage for the job

◆ fair to the individual

◆ more or less the best they can offer.

There is no conscious effort to make a low offer to save money or get a bargain by hiring a candidate cheaply. They believe in paying people adequately for the job and that, if they do not, they are at risk of losing their people to competition.

What this means for salary negotiations
Such companies can view salary and offer negotiation as unpleasant, distasteful or even bad manners. When dealing with a company with this approach, excessive attempts to bargain over salary are usually viewed poorly.

Opening offers

A company making opening offers tends to have the view that negotiation over salaries on joining the company is perfectly normal and expected. This may either be a company attitude, or just the viewpoint of the manager hiring you.

How offers are arrived at
Companies which expect you to try to negotiate a higher salary with them are highly unlikely to make you their best offer straight away, are they? They may be trying to get a bargain, by trying to employ people at as low a cost as possible, but this is not always the case. Often, they have experienced making what they believe to be a fair offer, in the past, and lost candidates who wanted to negotiate a higher sum which they could not afford.

Basically, an initial offer might be based on:

◆ The lowest amount they think they could get away with.

◆ The bottom figure of the salary quoted in an advert.

◆ The same amount you are being paid in your current job.

What this means for salary negotiations
Whatever the figure, this is unlikely to be their real offer; it is simply an opening offer which they expect you to respond to. Their idea is that they will negotiate and achieve a salary that both sides think is fair. Failure to negotiate with a company like this means that you will sell yourself short, and also potentially lose respect from your new boss before you even start.

How can you tell which offer it is?
With one approach, the offer is fair and probably not negotiable by much, if at all. Trying to negotiate may be

viewed negatively. With the other approach the offer is negotiable, and negotiation is fully expected. *Not* negotiating may be viewed negatively. So how can you tell which is the case?

By research. Before you got to this stage you should have gathered salary information. So when you are told the salary offer, you will know whether it is fair or not – do your homework, it's that simple.

Sources of salary information

◆ If you came via an agency, the agency must have had some idea of likely salary.

◆ If you responded to an advert, that will probably have shown a salary or range for the job advertised.

◆ You should check with online recruitment sites, papers and magazines, and agencies for typical salaries for the job in question.

Company concerns about candidates

Believe it or not, some companies do have worries of their own when making a job offer. They have their own concerns about you, and how the offer will be perceived by you. Others don't have the same concerns, but it is useful to see how their thinking sometimes works.

◆ Some companies are concerned that if they offer too low a salary they may look bad, and it could affect their reputation in the marketplace. This is especially true if they are considering a candidate currently working at a rival company, a competitor or even a client of their company.

◆ If a company is still concerned about whether or not you would actually take the job, they may be nervous of making the offer. They may well have had their fingers burnt in the past by making an offer which a candidate then went on to use as a bargaining tool internally, to secure a pay rise with their current employer!

THE MOST COMMON MISTAKES IN SALARY NEGOTIATIONS

Most employers will not discuss the issue of pay until they have decided to hire you. It is important you do the same.

Lack of preparation

◆ Showing your current salary on your CV or an application form.

◆ Not researching market salaries for the type of work concerned.

◆ Not having the facts – not knowing your current salary and benefits details.

◆ Not knowing what you are worth.

◆ Not knowing what you want or need to earn.

Incorrect attitudes

◆ Assuming that the employer will know the fair salary for the job.

◆ Assuming that salaries are predetermined by employers, so there's no point trying to negotiate.

◆ Thinking that just because you've been offered the job now, the employer won't change their mind.

◆ Thinking that if they have offered you the job, negotiation will be easy as they won't want to lose you.

◆ Being greedy.

◆ Taking things personally – a salary should be for a job, not a person.

◆ Feeling embarrassed about negotiating – it's natural to feel that way and the employer probably feels embarrassed too!

Giving away too much information

◆ Not knowing how to handle questions about salary.

◆ Giving away too much information.

◆ Giving a single figure when asked what salary expectations you have.

◆ Telling the employer about your needs, not theirs.

◆ Not establishing your *value* before you discuss your *worth*.

◆ Prematurely discussing salary before gaining information on the job requirements, or before communicating your qualifications and value to employers.

◆ Lying about your current or previous salary.

◆ Saying yes or no straight away.

Lack of skills or experience

◆ Not knowing how to negotiate.

◆ Not understanding benefits as part of a compensation package.

◆ Projecting an image that isn't in line with the salary you want.

◆ Negotiating salary or benefits by telephone.

◆ Being too quick to accept an initial offer.

◆ Being afraid to take your time, or to use timing to increase your value.

◆ Not allowing room for negotiation.

PRINCIPLES OF SALARY NEGOTIATION

Always establish worth before discussing value

Your worth to the company is what you will bring them – what they will gain from employing you. You have a unique combination of skills and experience and personality. Your value is what you will cost. Throughout this book we have advocated not discussing salary during interviews until you are sure the company wants to hire you. This is about establishing your worth to them before they try to put a price tag on you.

Your personal circumstances are not relevant

Here's a hard point to take on board. You may know that you have a large mortgage, or that your childminder costs £7,000 a year – but the employer isn't interested in that. Don't ever bring personal circumstances into the discussion. It introduces problems, and the employer doesn't need to know you have problems – keep everything focused on positive issues.

The only exception to this is the subject of travelling – or anything else if it already forms part of your package outside your current salary and so needs taking into account. If, for example, your current job pays you a travel allowance or reimbursement in addition to your salary, and therefore this needs to be factored into any new salary, you will need to bring this up at some stage.

The first number mentioned

The first number mentioned can often determine the range within which any negotiation or bargaining will take place. Employers or hiring managers usually have an amount in mind that they are thinking of offering you, but they will very often try to get you to name a number first.

Never go first

If asked what salary you were thinking of, you could end up in trouble! If you answer too high, you could disqualify yourself for the role – the employer may think there's no point making you an offer anyway. If your answer is too low, you devalue yourself.

How to avoid giving a figure

The only real way to avoid giving a figure is by not answering the question in some way! Common sense tells you that 'I'm sorry I'd rather not answer that' is a pretty bad answer, and not likely to get the job. The best possible answer is as follows:

'I am much more interested in (type of work) here at (name of company) than I am in the size of the *initial* offer.'

Why is this so good?

◆ You focus on your interest in the job, not the money.

◆ You tell them you want to work for them – without grovelling.

◆ Most candidates will say a figure, whereas you tell them how much you like the idea of working for them.

◆ It manages to avoid answering the question with a number.

A lot of the time an employer will be happy with this, and go on to make you an offer without further discussion. But obviously different people have different personalities and different ways of doing things. So if the answer sounds totally alien to you, try one of these alternatives:

◆ What did you have in mind?

◆ Did you have a figure in mind you wanted to bounce off me?

◆ A reasonable offer – money isn't always the main motivator for me.

◆ I don't have a firm figure in mind, but I'm sure it would be within the range you stated in the advert.

◆ Quite frankly I really like the sound of this role, so I'm open to offer.

◆ It depends on the benefits and total package, but money isn't the main issue here, I want a role I can really get satisfaction from/get my teeth into/practise my skills in/learn from (or any other reason you feel is more appropriate).

If forced to give a figure
Remember advice in previous chapters. Here are some ideas:

◆ Never give a figure, give a range.

◆ Then follow it with the question, 'Does that fit with your own thoughts?' to try to see whether you're in the right area.

Know your bottom line
This is the minimum amount you can accept for the job.

Ways of handling tricky questions
There are a number of tricky questions you may encounter about salary. Here are some suggestions for how to handle them.

'What's your current salary?'

◆ 'I'd prefer to discuss the position in more detail before looking at salary issues.'

◆ 'Can I come back to that when you have a better picture of what I have to offer?'

'How much do you think you are worth?'

◆ 'I am looking for the maximum, fair salary for the responsibilities involved in the job I'm asked to do.'

'What do you expect the salary range of this position to be?'

◆ 'Is this a job offer?'

◆ 'I'm not sure – what range did you have in mind?'

◆ 'I'm sure you pay fairly – it isn't a concern for me at this stage.'

PREPARING TO NEGOTIATE YOUR TERMS

Many people find negotiating an offer uncomfortable, so it is wise to prepare in order to make it easier. The process should be relatively smooth, and how well it goes will depend on how well you (and the employer, but you can only control your side) get round the barriers that are bound to come up between you. Preparation is everything.

Build up a relationship

Show enthusiasm

You will need to make sure they know how excited you feel

about the job. Spend a little time making sure you can put that across.

Make them feel good

Listening carefully to the other person helps build rapport and hence the relationship. This is especially important if the person is potentially your new boss. Listening involves not interrupting and allowing them to finish their thoughts, as well as repeating back to that person a part of what they've said in the course of your answer so that they know they've been heard. Additionally, things such as establishing good eye contact, nodding after a statement to reinforce that you've heard it, etc. are common communication devices that say: 'I heard you and I understand what you're saying.'

Make it easy for them

You want to give the overall message that you want to work for them, it's just the salary/money issue that needs to be resolved. This makes it clear that you're both on the same side trying to resolve a common problem, not on opposing ones.

Practise what to say

◆ Avoid being confrontational.

◆ Be polite and reasonable.

HANDLING THE SURPRISE NEGOTIATION

If you attend what you thought would be an interview or meeting, and are suddenly made a job offer or asked to consider a hypothetical offer, this can be a pretty big surprise. Coping with this can be hard, as you feel caught out and unprepared. Here are some good suggestions for how to respond.

Your four options

In a way your options aren't that complicated, as you only have four of them:

◆ stall for more time to think

◆ accept the offer

◆ reject the offer

◆ negotiate the offer.

STALLING FOR TIME

Don't panic

There is no reason to accept an offer immediately, and fortunately most organisations will not expect you to accept an offer on the spot.

Express your appreciation

If you are going to ask for more time, make sure that the first thing you do is to express appreciation for the offer.

Explain the need for more time

Explain to the employer that this is an important decision, and that you would therefore like some more time to think about it.

Agree on a reasonable time frame

Agree with them the time and date by which you will get back to them with your answer.

Ask any questions

Ask any questions necessary in order to understand the offer completely, then leave politely. There is no point in staying any longer – if you are too positive they may think you will accept the offer, which may reduce your bargaining power later. If you are cautious they may assume you won't accept it, and try to persuade you, which can be awkward.

Asking for it in writing

You can try this, but nowadays it is becoming rare for companies to issue an offer unless they already have a verbal acceptance.

DEALING WITH UNFAVOURABLE OFFERS – REJECTION AND NEGOTIATION

Managing your instant reaction

So you've been made an offer and you don't much like it. What happens now? The first and most important thing is to manage your instant reaction.

Manage your anxiety

You may well feel anxious doing this. Many candidates are concerned that the employer will change his or her mind about hiring you, just because you aren't eager to take their first offer. Just remember the facts:

◆ Don't worry – they obviously like you.

◆ You must be someone they want to hire, or they wouldn't be making you an offer.

◆ If there is only one job available, you must be first choice to be sitting where you are now.

◆ Going back to a second or even third choice candidate will cost them time and money – many employers will find it easier to strike an acceptable deal with you than go back to the drawing board.

Things not to say

◆ 'Thank you' – it's an offer you don't like, so don't imply you're grateful.

◆ 'Okay' – it means 'yes', or 'it's acceptable' to most people and gives the impression the offer is okay – which of course it isn't.

◆ It should go without saying, but don't be rude or laugh!

What you should say

The routine
This is going to sound silly to some people, but practise the following simple technique until it looks and sounds completely natural:

◆ say nothing . . .

◆ find a useful noise you can make such as hmmm, uh-huh, mmmm . . .

- if you can't feel comfortable doing that, just repeat the figure they quoted quietly but audibly to yourself and say nothing else

- and look down

- pause and count to three . . .

- then look back at the person who made the offer as if you expect them to say something else.

What it means
This little routine will be very false to some people. Let's see why it is so important in creating the right impression psychologically.

Your overall stance
The impression you need to give is that:

- you hear and understand what they've said, *but*

- it is making you uncomfortable/unhappy/disappointed *and*

- you're too polite and professional to tell them that just yet . . .

Why is this the impression you want to give? Because it invites *them* to ask *you* what is going on, inducing them to make the first move. Think about the process here: they have just made an offer, and if you say you're not happy with it, you are rejecting them. *You* are making the first move out of the comfort zone. By indirectly implying you're unhappy, most employers will respond by asking you about it, which

Step	What it means and suggests to the employer
Say nothing.	Remember saying 'okay' or 'yes' or 'thank you' will give the wrong message.
Find a useful noise you can make such as hmmm, uh-huh, mmm . . . If you can't feel comfortable doing that, just repeat the figure they quoted quietly but audibly to yourself.	This shows them that you did actually hear them – staying silent might make them wonder if you heard what they said!
Say nothing else.	This creates a gap in the conversation. Most people are uncomfortable with pauses and will try to fill them by saying something. If you don't, the chances are that they will . . .
Look down.	This *implies* unhappiness/ discomfort/lack of agreement with that they said, without saying so outright.
Pause and count to three.	Make that pause a little longer – it suggests you are thinking, and counting to three lengthens the pause a little longer, which may make them want to fill the silence.
Look back at the person who made the offer expectantly.	If they still haven't said anything, look at them as if you fully expect them to and they usually will.

makes *them* make the first move towards a compromise. It means *you* haven't asked *them* to negotiate, *they* asked *you.*

What if they don't respond?

You have set up the situation to induce them to negotiate. If they don't, what do you do then? You can't both sit there in silence! It's simple – just say, 'I'm sorry, were you looking for an immediate response, because that figure was very unexpected?'

This implies yet again that you are disappointed, without actually saying that, and they will usually respond, saying 'Why?' This now gives you a chance to explain what *your* idea of an offer was, and suddenly, you're negotiating!

Negotiating

What do you do if you have just been offered your dream job, but at a disappointingly low salary? Well, only you know the answer to that one! It depends on your bottom line, how much you want the job, whether or not you feel there's any room for negotiation. Negotiation is probably your best idea here. Having tried the above routine, and now you and the employer are in a conversation, how do you negotiate that offer? These steps will help:

◆ Express your appreciation for the offer.

◆ Express your enthusiasm for the job, but . . .

◆ Ask whether or not there is any flexibility regarding the salary.

◆ Listen carefully to the response, because it will give you an idea of whether or not it's worthwhile to pursue the issue.

◆ If the salary itself cannot be increased, ask when the next review will be and request a salary review after, say, six months.

◆ Don't make any decision on financial grounds alone, unless the offer is below your bottom line.

Rejecting an offer (in person)

Sometimes you will want to reject an offer outright. It depends on the situation, how much you want the job, the rapport and relationship you have built up with the interviewer(s) – a range of factors. If you wish to do this, try this technique.

◆ Express your appreciation for the gesture of confidence in you which they are making.

◆ Find something positive and diplomatic to say.

◆ Tell them that unfortunately it isn't acceptable to you, and apologise that things haven't worked out.

◆ If they respond with some discussion or negotiation, always be prepared to negotiate – but be prepared to still say no eventually if necessary. Keep an open mind.

◆ Unless they respond with anything else, such as a revised offer or discussion, you need to leave politely.

An example

Jane was asked to a final interview for a job described in the job advert as paying £25,000 to £28,000. Jane earned £25,000, and had outgrown her role and was looking for something more senior, which was a good description of the job she was interviewing for. The interviewers already knew her current salary (obviously she hadn't read this book yet).

In the final interview, after about 30 minutes of questions and discussions with her potential boss and two other senior managers, the interviewers suddenly looked at each other, nodded and came out with a surprise.

'We have some good news,' one of them said, 'we'd like to offer you the job.'

'Thank you,' said Jane, 'I'm delighted.'

'Yes,' the interviewer continued, 'the salary would be £25,000 to start, rising annually to the maximum of £28,000.'

'I'm sorry,' said Jane, 'it appears we have been wasting each others' time. I know you're aware I already earn that in my current role, and that has far less responsibility than you are looking for me to take here. I hope you also realise that I really liked the idea of working for you – this job would have been perfect for my next move. I apologise for the way things have turned out, but there's no way I would be able to accept that figure for your role here.' And she started to stand up to leave.

What do you think happened next? Actually, she got the job at £28,000, but that's not important. What *is* important is that she was polite, and made the employers aware of how she felt, but at the same time she was firm and very nicely rejected the offer. This was a case of an offer rejection that turned quickly into a negotiation.

Had the situation not changed, she should have left the interview politely, shaking hands and saying goodbye with each one, and then written to them to confirm the conversation. Actually, sometimes this also gets results – by writing to them it confirms your decision and sometimes the employer will ask you back to discuss a revised offer.

DEALING WITH FAVOURABLE OFFERS – ACCEPTING A JOB OFFER (IN PERSON)

Okay, so you've been offered the job, on a salary that is acceptable to you. You want to say yes, don't you? But why not wait a little, just in case?

Don't accept immediately

Obviously this depends on the situation. Sometimes the offer is good, the job is perfect and you know this company doesn't negotiate – so say yes! For other situations, try this instead:

◆ No matter how good the offer is, don't accept it right away.

◆ Show your appreciation of the offer.

◆ Say that you're very interested and excited about the opportunity and will get back to them in 24 hours.

◆ You might even ask to have a little more time to get back to them, especially if you are in the process of interviewing and have already made other appointments.

◆ Ask if you can make a note of the main points.

◆ Ask them about other benefits you might be entitled to such as:
—health insurance
—holidays
—annual salary review
—pensions
—bonus schemes.

◆ Tell them you will think it over and get back to them quickly.

◆ Be prepared to reassure them if they seem disappointed by this, by reinforcing how excited and pleased you are.

◆ If you really don't need to wait 24 hours, say you'd be delighted to accept, subject to written confirmation of the offer and terms/conditions.

◆ Don't ruin things by being too grateful and grovelling!

DEALING WITH OFFERS OF ALTERNATIVE JOBS

Very occasionally you get invited to a meeting and are given 'good news and bad news'. You haven't got the job, but they do like you and they have another job opening they'd like to offer you instead.

Lesser jobs

Is this good news? It all depends on whether or not you like the new job that's on offer. You may be offered a job that is lesser; for example, you may be offered a clerical assistant role instead of the administrator role you applied for.

Sometimes this is acceptable, sometimes not. Here are the factors you need to carefully weigh up, and then respond just as with any other offer.

◆ What does the job involve? If the work is substantially different from the job you applied for, is it something for which you would have applied? You don't have to be grateful for anything you're offered! You *must* ask about the job itself before the salary, to show your interest, not your disappointment and suspicion!

◆ What is the salary? You need to know this, but never ask before you have asked about the job itself. You don't want to give the impression you are motivated by money, or make a decision financially before you have all the facts.

◆ It can also sometimes be useful to know *why* they have offered you this job and not the other. Maybe they really liked you but someone else was better – this is no reflection on you, as they liked you enough to want to hire you anyway.

CHECKLIST

◆ Try to ascertain the company's approach to job offers. You may get a feel for this during the interview process, or if you're unlucky you may have to decide based on the offer they make.

◆ Never ever reveal 'your number' first. It will only ever weaken your position.

◆ Learn and practise routines to get you out of awkward situations.

◆ Prepare in advance, so that you can react and respond effectively even in unexpected situations.

◆ Never be afraid to stall for time, or even ask directly for it.

◆ Ensure you are practised and at ease dealing with unfavourable offers.

9

Answering Tough Questions

There are a large number of books available on answering interview questions. The purpose of this section is not to duplicate them, but to explain in general what you should try to put across in answer to some of the questions. If you know what you want to put across, you can then choose your own form of words that sounds and feels right for you, and fits your own style and personality. After all, there's nothing worse than learning words from a book and then trying to remember what to say under pressure.

You won't find many suggested answers here, but this chapter aims to give you a good overview of questions and what information the recruiter is looking or hoping for. This should enable you to think of your own answers.

GENERAL ADVICE FOR ANSWERING QUESTIONS

Listen and understand

◆ Listen to the question.

◆ Ask for clarification if you don't understand.

◆ If the interviewer speaks too fast or has an accent, don't be afraid to ask them to repeat the question.

Control your nerves

◆ Remember that nerves or stress can have an effect on your voice.

◆ Don't speak too quickly or too slowly when answering.

◆ Don't ramble on – keep answers to the point, and relatively brief.

Help the interviewer out

◆ Always remember – not all interviewers are expert. You may have to try to give them the information they want, if they don't ask for it themselves.

◆ Don't take questions literally – it usually leads to one-word answers.

◆ Don't give yes or no answers – expand slightly without giving too long an answer.

QUESTION SUBJECTS

There are literally thousands of questions that you could be asked in an interview. Here are some of the main question types classified by what the interviewer is looking for.

Behavioural questions or competency-based questions

These are questions aimed at eliciting examples of past performance. They usually ask for examples of past situations you have been in, what happened, and how you reacted or behaved. These will be covered in full in the next chapter.

Examples

◆ Can you tell me about a time when . . .

◆ Can you give me an example of . . .

◆ Tell me about an instance when you were in that sort of situation and what happened.

Motivation questions

These are questions that are trying to find out your motivation – to discover more about what drives you. By this we mean your motivation for doing this job, for this company, your motivation for leaving your current job, whatever. They tend to be the 'why?' questions.

Examples

◆ Why do you want to work for this company?

◆ Why are you interested in working for us?

◆ Why have you applied for this job?

◆ Do you prefer detailed work, or work where you can explore options? (Why?)

◆ Do you prefer working alone or in groups? (Why?)

◆ How ambitious are you?

◆ What are your long-term career aspirations?

◆ Where do you see yourself in five years?

◆ How ambitious would you say you are?

◆ What are your greatest strengths?

◆ What would you say are your greatest weaknesses?

Hints and tips

Give positive reasons wherever possible. These are called 'pull factors' – things that motivate you *towards* them. Avoid talking about 'push factors' – these are things that motivate you *away from* them if possible (unless you're specifically asked). 'Towards motivation' is more positive and likely to be more genuine and well thought out. For example:

◆ Say: 'I'd like to work here because you have an excellent reputation, and you can offer me an increased challenge, wider experience and opportunities to develop my career.'

◆ Not: 'I'd like to work here because I'm not happy in my current job, and it's really time for me to make a move if I want to get more experience and develop my career.'

In the above example you can see the difference between 'towards' and 'away from' motivation quite clearly. The 'towards motivation' sounds far more attractive to an employer.

If asked about your motivation to work for the company or do the job, show enthusiasm and interest in it. Show the interviewer how much research you've done. Let them know what you think you can bring to the company.

Avoid saying anything too negative. If asked about a weakness or anything that requires a negative answer, always balance it with a positive, for example:

◆ 'My greatest weakness would have to be deadlines, so I have a system of To Do lists which I've developed over the years. I update my lists every day, to make sure tasks and deadlines are all accounted for and factored into my priorities. I've found it works for me in all my jobs, and it means I never miss a deadline any more!'

Challenging questions

These are questions that challenge your skills, abilities, experience, knowledge.

Examples

◆ Why should we hire you?

◆ What do you feel you have to offer this role?

◆ What parts of the job do you feel you would have most trouble with?

◆ What can you offer us that someone else can't?

◆ Your experience seems light for this role – what do you think?

Hints and tips

These questions usually make most people feel on the defensive, so it is important not to react to them instinctively. Remember that it is not a personal attack, the interviewer is simply trying to home in on one area in detail. Try to turn the question round into an opportunity to shine.

If you feel defensive, remember not to let these questions reduce your confidence. They chose to interview you, so you must have enough relevant skills and abilities to make it worth their time interviewing you.

Demonstration questions

These are questions which ask you to demonstrate how you do things. They are a little like behavioural or competency-based questions, but rather than being phrased as a question which asks for a specific example, they leave the question more open.

Examples

◆ How do you cope under stress?

◆ How ambitious are you?

◆ How do you react to criticism?

◆ How good are you at detailed work?

Hints and tips

These are basically behavioural or competency-based questions badly phrased. For example, by 'how do you cope under stress?' the interviewer probably means 'can you give me an example of when you have coped under a lot of stress?' Because the question is phrased badly, it enables candidates to hypothesise and make up a good answer about how well they behave under stress, without any evidence to back it up.

The best idea is to answer with an example, as if this were a competency-based question.

Example: 'how do you cope under stress?'

◆ Answer: 'well, the last time I faced this was when . . . and I responded by . . . and now I find that when my stress levels get very high this technique usually works. I just take a few deep breaths, and set myself a deadline to work towards, after which I take a short break to clear my head.'

◆ Not: 'I take some deep breaths and take a break as soon as I can.'

Information questions

These questions are simply factual questions, designed to gain additional facts and data.

Examples

◆ What do you dislike doing?

◆ What magazines and newspapers do you read?

◆ What do you do to keep yourself up to date in your field?

Hints and tips

Answer these questions factually, and keep it short – the interviewer may have a number of facts he or she wishes to check, so long answers mean they cannot ask all the questions they would like. In any event, this type of question really doesn't warrant a long answer. At the same time avoid one- or two-word answers, such as 'nothing,' or '*The Times*'. Make the answer into a short sentence.

QUESTION TYPES

There are several different ways of asking for the same information. Understanding the types of question you might face can help you think on your feet and come up with good answers.

Closed questions

Closed questions are questions that give you very little room to respond. The question is phrased in such a way as to limit your answer.

Examples

◆ How many staff were in the team?

◆ How long did you work there?

◆ What grade did you get for the exam?

◆ What was you job title?

How to respond

They have asked a question that asks for a very specific piece of information. Don't therefore give them a great, long, rambling answer. Answer the question and expand if necessary, to at most one or two sentences.

Example: 'how many staff were in the team?'

◆ Answer: There were four staff in the team, plus myself and the manager.

◆ Not: Four.

Yes/no questions

These are like closed questions but require only a yes/no answer. Inexperienced interviewers tend to use them in error.

Examples

◆ Do you have a degree?

◆ Have you resigned yet?

◆ Do you like that type of work?

◆ Are you good under pressure?

◆ Are you very ambitious?

◆ Do you respond well to aggressive or difficult customers?

Hints and tips

Although all these questions can be answered with a simple yes or no, the interviewer is probably not looking for that. Also, although a simple yes or no might be appropriate for one or two questions, if the interviewer has a number of these, then answering just yes or no all the time will make you appear to be a poor communicator.

Finally, giving yes or no answers doesn't give you any chance to shine – it means you don't offer your good qualities and examples to the interviewer.

Example: 'are you good under pressure?'

◆ Answer: 'Yes, I've been under pressure recently regarding . . . and I managed to keep everything in order by . . .'

◆ Not: 'Yes.'

Hypothetical questions

These questions ask you to imagine what you would do in a given situation. They are actually very poor questioning technique, because they allow the worst candidates to imagine how good they might be at something, and then talk about that. It means their faults are never exposed.

Examples

◆ Imagine you are on the phone and likely to be some time, when an angry customer walks in and wants to talk to you right now – even though you are on the phone. What would you do?

◆ What would you do if you had responsibility for that area?

How to respond

You have two choices really. If you have been in that situation before, you can use this as an example. If the example went badly you can still use it if you like, but make it positive by saying how you would behave differently now.

◆ For example: 'Well, that happened to me once, and how I handled it was by . . . Of course, now I've seen how that went I might change my approach slightly and . . .'

Secondly, if you have never been in that situation before, you can only hypothesise – which is basically making something up! This is why these questions aren't very good – having candidates guess how they might react isn't a very good predictor of how they might behave in the job. If you face this sort of question, make your guess relevant to the job – forcing the interviewer to actually picture you doing the job.

◆ For example: I've never been in this situation, but assuming I was successful and working for you, I think I'd handle it like this . . .

Funnel questions

These are also called probing questions. They are not actually one question but a sequence of them, where the interviewer probes more and more deeply into something by a series of questions.

Examples

◆ What IT experience have you had? What software packages? What spreadsheets? How often have you used them? To what level?

◆ Your previous roles had all been in accounts – what made you decide to move into administration? Why did you decide to move just then? What sort of personal reasons?

◆ You say you like organising events – what sort of events have you organised? What was the largest? Who else helped organise it? So were you in charge? What specifically was your involvement?

How to respond
They attempt to pin you down, and this can make you feel very uncomfortable, even cornered and intimidated. If you do have any areas on your CV or application that have been embellished in any way, they may be exposed by this line of questioning. Be aware of these questions and how they are likely to make you feel. This may make it a little easier to stay positive and focused and not feel intimidated.

CHECKLIST

◆ Understand the purpose of questions so that you can react appropriately.

◆ Remember that not all interviewers are expert – you may need to help them out by offering the information they are trying to gain.

◆ Use positive language wherever possible.

◆ If you have to use a negative response or example, balance it with a positive, or give it a positive ending by mentioning what you learned from it.

◆ Understand the type of questions you may face, to structure good answers to poorly phrased questions.

10

Competency-Based Questions

WHAT ARE COMPETENCIES?

Competency-based interviewing is sometimes called **behavioural interviewing** or **situational interviewing**. This is where the interviewer asks you to describe examples of situations (hence the term situational interviewing) you have been in, and how you behaved (hence the term behavioural interviewing). The aim of the questions is to get you to give the interviewer evidence of certain characteristics or **competencies** that the organisation wants. Competencies are simply characteristics – the knowledge, skills, abilities and behaviours that you use to do a job. The idea is that the employer knows what competencies they are looking for, and during the interview process they use questioning to assess whether or not you have those competencies.

Typical competencies for an organisation will obviously vary widely. Here are some ideas of typical competencies a company might have decided are essential to do a job, and what they mean.

Communication

◆ Clarifying messages where necessary.

◆ Expressing needs, wants, opinions and preferences.

◆ Giving feedback.

◆ Listening with objectivity.

◆ Not causing conflict.

◆ Not offending others.

◆ Receiving feedback effectively.

Critical thinking

◆ Ability to see the 'big picture'.

◆ Being able to think in abstract terms.

◆ Critically evaluating data.

◆ Identifying and defining problems.

◆ Identifying probable causes.

◆ Making decisions.

◆ Making suggestions for a solution.

◆ Making judgements factually.

Ethics/social responsibility

◆ Considering the impact of actions and decisions on others, both inside and outside the company.

◆ Defining and practising ethical behaviour in difficult situations.

Team work

◆ Acknowledging other team members' concerns and contributions.

◆ Active participation in the team.

◆ Behaving in the best interests of the team.

◆ Being aware of the effect of behaviour on others.

◆ Collaborating on projects.

Technical knowledge

◆ Demonstrating satisfactory levels of technical and professional skills.

◆ Devising new solutions to problems based on technical or professional principles.

◆ Keeping abreast of current developments and trends in technical areas.

◆ Knowing where to get in-depth expertise on specific technical areas.

◆ Knowing how and when to apply skill or procedure.

◆ Understanding technical terminology and developments.

HOW DO COMPETENCY-BASED INTERVIEWS WORK?

Competency-based interviews consist of a series of questions designed to get you to give the interviewer behavioural information against specific job-related competencies. By behavioural information, we mean information on how you behaved – i.e. an example of what you did in a situation.

Information, usually in the form of specific examples of your past behaviour, is gathered against each competency that is relevant for that job, i.e. the aspects of personality, skill and motivation that are necessary for excellent job performance.

Why use competency-based interviews?

Quite simply, the theory is that the best predictor of future performance is past performance. Therefore, by gathering examples of how you behaved in previous situations, the interviewer can predict how you would work in the job.

Positive and negative questions

Questions can be phrased to look for either a positive or negative example. You could still use either, but you will usually be asked for one of only two things – an example of things going well (positive), or an example of when something didn't (negative).

Whichever way you are asked, and whether you give a positive or negative example, you must show yourself in a positive light. So if asked for a negative example, always finish by saying how you retrieved the situation, or put things right. If nothing else, describe what you learned from it.

◆ For example: 'so unfortunately, it really was my fault. The only good thing was that it taught me never to use only one supplier quote, and to make sure that I always check before signing the order delivery notes. That way, it won't happen again.'

EXAMPLE QUESTIONS

Remember that questions can either be phrased to look for a positive example, or a negative!

Positive examples

◆ Describe a time when you achieved something even though you didn't really think you could do it.

◆ Describe a situation where you used negotiating or persuasion to convince someone of your idea.

◆ How do you tend to deal with conflict at work – give me an example of when you've faced a difference of opinion with someone?

◆ Give me a situation where you had to achieve an important goal and were in danger of not doing it.

◆ Describe a time when you had too many tasks to do and had to prioritise to meet deadlines.

◆ Describe the most difficult decision you've had to make this year.

◆ Give me an example or two of when you've had to make a split-second decision, without time to plan or research the outcome.

[handwritten: ≫ peer mentor]

◆ Tell me about a time when you dealt with someone who was very upset.

Negative examples

◆ Tell me about a time when you've had to work with someone you really didn't like. *[handwritten: → One volunteer @ Boots]*

◆ Describe a time when you failed to meet a deadline. *[handwritten: → hasn't happened yet thankfully]*

◆ Describe the most stressful situation you have been in. *[handwritten: → work or general?]*

◆ Give me an example of when you've missed an important deadline and what you did to rectify the situation. *[handwritten: → n/a]*

◆ Tell me about a time when you've overlooked something *[handwritten: → n/a]* and had to backtrack as a result.

◆ Can you give an example of a time when you've tried to *[handwritten: → n/a]* achieve something but still failed?

◆ What's the most unpopular thing you've had to do? *[handwritten: ⇒]*

ADVICE FOR COMPETENCY-BASED INTERVIEWS

If you've never been in that situation

◆ If you have never been in the situation before, say so.

◆ Never just make something up without being asked to.

◆ Try, 'sorry, I've never been in that situation. I could imagine my response if you like' or 'would you like me to imagine it?'

◆ Try, 'sorry, I can't remember ever being in that situation, but I did face something slightly similar that I could discuss.'

If you can't think of anything

◆ Never just say, 'sorry, I can't think of anything.'

◆ Think laterally. Check your memory for social situations, school or even family examples.

◆ Ask for more time.

◆ If you still can't think of anything, ask if you can come back to the question later.

If the example that comes to mind ended in disaster!

◆ If you've been asked for a negative example, fine, give it.

◆ If asked for a positive example, preface your example by warning that it didn't end well: 'well, this didn't actually work out the way I planned, but it illustrates the point pretty well, and I did learn a lot from it. The situation was that . . .'

◆ Always end with a positive – what you learnt from it, what steps you put in place to prevent reoccurrence etc.

If you can think of several examples

◆ Choose the one that illustrates you in the best possible light.

◆ Choose the work-related one if there is one, rather than one involving, say, family or social activities.

◆ Choose the one most relevant to the job in question.

◆ Ask permission to answer the question slightly differently, if it will show you in a better light and be more relevant. The following example is better, for instance, than telling the interviewer about pre-wedding nerves.

Example: 'tell me about the most stressful situation you've faced in the last year'

◆ Answer: 'well that would have been my wedding, but almost as stressful was a major contract which we lost at work last month. Although it wasn't my fault I do feel responsible for taking some action to put right the things that led to that happening . . .'

A RELIABLE METHOD FOR STRUCTURING ANSWERS
Structure your answers with the mnemonic **SERL**: situation, effect, response, learnings. But don't be *too* long-winded – a sentence or two on each step is plenty.

Situation
Describe the situation in enough detail so that the interviewer can see it's relevant. You don't need to say a large amount or describe the incident or situation in detail.

Example

◆ 'Well, I was working in my last job when a customer complained that I hadn't dealt with their query properly.'

Effect

Describe the effects the situation had — on you, on the company etc.

Example

◆ 'This was actually quite serious, as we were in danger of losing the customer's business, and also if I *had* mishandled their query I would have been in big trouble!'

Response

Describe how you responded — what you did, what you organised, the changes you made.

Example

◆ 'It was just my word against hers, so as there was no evidence to prove that I had done everything by the book, I had to work on re-establishing my relationship with her, so she could be persuaded she was wrong. I apologised, and took the time to explain that I had actually done everything I could, but things had still not been to her liking. I offered to be her personal point of contact from now on.'

Learnings

Describe what you learnt from the experience – especially important if the example was a negative one, but a good idea even in positive situations.

Example

◆ 'She agreed, and the complaint was withdrawn. It was a useful experience really (although really unpleasant and worrying at the time), because I learnt that even if I'm not in the wrong, sometimes just saying sorry and making the first move can change things.'

CHECKLIST

◆ Understand what competencies are.

◆ Give positive examples wherever possible.

◆ If forced to give a negative example, make sure you show what you learned from the experience.

◆ Plan how to react if you can't find an example.

◆ Remember the SERL model for structuring your responses.

Helpful Addresses

Equal Opportunites Commission
Overseas House
Quay Street
Manchester M3 3HN
Tel: (0161) 833 9244
http://www.eoc.org.uk

Commission for Racial Equality
Elliott House
10–12 Allington Street
London SW1E 5EH
Tel: (020) 7828 7022
http://www.cre.gov.uk

Disability Rights Commission
2nd Floor
Arndale House
The Arndale Centre
Manchester M4 3AQ
Tel: (08457) 622633
Textphone (for people with hearing difficulties) (08457)
    622644
http://www.drc-gb.org

Recruitment and Employment Confederation
Tel: (020) 7462 3260
http://www.rec.uk.com/

Further Reading

Secrets of Successful Interviewing, Dorothy Leeds (Piatkus).

30 Minutes Before Your Job Interview, June Lines (Kogan Page).

30 Minutes to Make the Right Impression, Eleri Sampson (Kogan Page).

Succeed at Your Job Interview, George Heaviside (BBC).

Great Answers to Tough Interview Questions, Martin John Yate (Kogan Page).

Write a Winning CV, Julie-Ann Amos (How To Books).

Index

age, 15
anxiety, 129
aptitude tests, 105, 106–107

beliefs, 15
body language, 24–26

case studies, 89–90
competencies, 45, 57, 81, 83, 94–97, 99, 105, 152–161
concerns of interviewers/ employers, 55–59, 66, 119
conflict, 88, 98
criminal records, 14

disability, 14
discrimination, 13
discussions, 95
dress, 20, 52

entrances, 22
ethnic origin, 15
exercises, group, 87, 96–98
exercises, individual, 88
exercises, leaderless, 97

honesty, 12
hostile interviewers, 60–62

interruptions, 93
in-tray exercises, 94

lying, 12

mirroring, 26

negative, 53, 143, 155, 157
nerves, 17, 61, 62, 141

panel interviews, 91–93
personality tests, 104, 108–111
pregnancy, 15
presentations, 99–100

race, 15
reception, 19, 52
refreshments, 23
religion, 15
research, 54, 119, 143

salary, 35, 46, 48, 69, 72–73, 75, 118–137
sexual orientation, 16
simulations, 93

weakness, 53, 143–144